The Implementation of the National **Numeracy** Strategy

The Final Report of the Numeracy Task Force

Published July 1998

Caerleon
Library

3

The Secretary of State for Education and Employment
Sanctuary Buildings
Great Smith Street
London
SW1P 3BT

Dear David

I am pleased to be able to submit to you our Final Report, *The Implementation of the National Numeracy Strategy,* which follows on from our Preliminary Report *Numeracy Matters.* Over the year we have been in existence, we have been greatly encouraged by the interest that we have found in numeracy amongst teachers, parents and educational organisations in general. We have also been greatly impressed by the positive way in which many diverse and distinctive groups, organisations and individuals responded to our statements in *Numeracy Matters* about those practices that we wish to encourage.

These respondents, the research evidence that we have studied, the ongoing effective programmes such as The National Numeracy Project, the evidence from OFSTED inspections, the experience of mathematics educators and the practices of other countries have all increasingly converged on a "solid centre" of agreed good practice in mathematics teaching, which our reports both reflect and then develop further.

With this Final Report, we outline to you the strategy which we believe to be necessary for the implementation of these kinds of practices throughout the schools, colleges, LEAs and homes of England.

We are grateful to you for the chance to help raise achievement significantly for all children.

Yours sincerely

David Reynolds

David Reynolds
Professor of Education, University of Newcastle upon Tyne
Chair of Numeracy Task Force
1st June 1998

Professor David Reynolds
Chair of Numeracy Task Force

24 June 1998

Dear David

Thank you for your letter of 1 June, enclosing the Numeracy Task Force's final report, *The Implementation of the National Numeracy Strategy.*

I am extremely grateful to you and your colleagues for the outstanding job you have done over the last year. I am also delighted to hear of the positive way in which teachers, parents and others in education have responded to your work and to the recommendations in your preliminary report.

I am pleased to accept in full the Task Force's recommendations for the implementation of the National Numeracy Strategy. The recommended strategy is an ambitious and practical programme for achieving our national target that, by 2002, 75% of 11 year olds will reach the level expected for children of their age. The strategy will affect every school with primary age pupils in the country. We shall provide training and support for all teachers to bring about the changes in teaching that the Task Force recommends, based on the good practice that it has identified.

Once again, I would like to thank the members of the Task Force for the important contribution they have made to raising standards for our children.

Best wishes

DAVID BLUNKETT

The Numeracy Task Force

Members

David Reynolds (Chair)	Professor of Education University of Newcastle
Martin Armstrong	Deputy Headteacher Marlwood School, South Gloucestershire
Margaret Brown	Professor of Mathematics Education King's College London
David Burghes	Professor of Education, Centre for Innovation in Mathematics Teaching University of Exeter
Margaret Dawes	KPMG
Pat Petch	Chair, National Governors' Council
Carol Robinson	Headteacher William Ford Church of England Junior School Barking and Dagenham
Chris Robson	Professor of Pure Mathematics University of Leeds
Anita Straker	Director, National Numeracy Project
Anne Waterhouse	Adviser, Lancashire County Council (formerly Headteacher, Asmall County Primary School Ormskirk, Lancashire).

Observers

Nigel Bufton	Office for Standards in Education (OFSTED)
Frankie Sulke	Teacher Training Agency (TTA)
Angela Walsh (until Nov 1997) Richard Browne (from Nov 1997)	Qualifications and Curriculum Authority (QCA)
Sandy Adamson	DfEE, Standards and Effectiveness Unit
Rosemary Pratt	DfEE, Standards and Effectiveness Unit
Dave Sleep	DfEE, Standards and Effectiveness Unit
Julian Critchley	DfEE, Curriculum and Assessment Division
Daniel Muijs	Research Associate, University of Newcastle
Barbara Tucker	DfEE, Standards and Effectiveness Unit (*minutes*)

Copies of this report and the Numeracy Task Force's preliminary report, *'Numeracy Matters'*, are available from the DfEE orderline on 0845 60 222 60.

CONTENTS

Page

Summary of Recommendations   2

Chapter 1
Consultation and the way ahead   6

Chapter 2
Training and support for schools   20

Chapter 3
The strategy in schools   50

Chapter 4
Creating a climate of support at home and in the wider community   74

Annex I
National Numeracy Strategy: Timetable of Key Events   86

Annex II
Funding the National Numeracy Strategy   89

Annex III
Recommendations   90

Summary of recommendations

The Task Force's final report gives a practical agenda for action to implement the National Numeracy Strategy, based on the wide support for the proposals in our preliminary report, *Numeracy Matters*, and taking into account the comments and concerns passed on to us during consultation. We have sought to make proposals that achieve good value for money within the funding likely to be available. We have focused in particular on the need to build up teachers' confidence and competence as quickly as possible at the beginning of the strategy. Our recommended strategy provides training and support for all teachers, to bring about changes in the teaching of mathematics in primary, middle and special school classrooms, reflecting the good practice identified in our preliminary report. The proposals and support build in particular on the National Numeracy Project (NNP).

The principles on which our report is based are set out in chapter 1, and recommendations set out in full at the end of each chapter. Our key recommendations are as follows:

1   From the autumn term 1999, all primary and special schools should teach a daily mathematics lesson to all pupils, lasting between 45 and 60 minutes depending on pupils' ages. Teachers should teach the whole class together for a high proportion of the lesson, and oral and mental work should feature strongly in each lesson.

2   LEAs should be funded to recruit numeracy consultants to support schools, and be given an early indication of how many are likely to be funded, so that they can recruit in the autumn term 1998 to begin work on 1 April 1999. The DfEE should also support the strategy with a national and regional infrastructure similar to that for the National Literacy Strategy.

3   The *Framework for teaching mathematics, Reception to Year 6*, to be referred to later in this report as either the *Framework for teaching* or simply 'the Framework', developed and used in the NNP, should be sent to all primary, special and secondary schools, LEAs and initial teacher training providers early in the spring term 1999. All primary and special schools should review their current practice and consider to what extent the teaching practices we recommend for the National Numeracy Strategy, and the *Framework for teaching* itself, suggest a need for change in their own school. The school's decision about the scale of change should be made in consultation with the LEA and the appropriate Regional Director for the strategy.

4   Particularly in the early stages of the strategy, consultants should be supplemented in giving demonstration lessons by skilled local teachers, whom we have termed "leading mathematics teachers". Both consultants and "leading mathematics teachers" should have training before fulfilling their roles.

5   All primary and special school teachers should have an opportunity, early in the autumn term 1999, to observe successful teaching of the daily mathematics lesson at least once using the strategy we have recommended. Demonstration lessons should be provided either by LEA numeracy consultants, local teachers identified as "leading mathematics teachers", or by good quality video material, showing relevant lessons, sent to all schools.

6   The available funding should be targeted mainly at providing training for teachers, including up to 5 days of release time for all primary and special schools, to allow teachers to watch demonstration lessons, and for the mathematics co-ordinator and the special educational needs co-ordinator (SENCO) to work with colleagues.

7   The headteacher, mathematics co-ordinator, and one other teacher (preferably the SENCO) from every primary and special school should attend an initial 3 day training conference in the summer term 1999, with a governor attending for the third day.

8   Every primary and special school should devote an INSET day in the summer term 1999, after the conference, to whole school training to prepare for planning and teaching the daily mathematics lesson. This should be followed up by two further INSET days, in the autumn term 1999 and spring term 2000. All the INSET should be supported by national training materials, especially high quality video of appropriate teaching methods. In the longer term, the DfEE should ensure attention to teachers' continuing professional development needs, especially in subject knowledge.

9   Schools identified by their LEA as needing intensive support - around 10 to 15 per cent of all primary and special schools in the first year of the strategy - should send the mathematics co-ordinator and one other teacher on a five day course, and receive up to six days of direct support from the local numeracy consultant. An additional 45% of schools should receive around 2 days of direct support from the consultant in the first year. Overall, intensive support should be given to up to around 60% of all schools in the course of the strategy. Intensive support should be available for up to 10% of all schools for two or even three years, if they are in particular need of it.

10 LEAs should agree numeracy targets for 2002 with the DfEE, and negotiate and agree targets for 2002 with their primary and special schools. They should identify someone with the management experience and mathematical skills to provide supportive line management and help with training for the LEA's numeracy consultants.

11 Special schools with pupils at Key Stages 1 and 2 should play a full part in the National Numeracy Strategy, adapting the structure of the daily lesson where necessary to take account of the particular needs of their pupils, and with supplementary training for teachers as needed.

12   Training and other guidance sent to all schools should take into account the need to help teachers teach the daily lesson with a high proportion of children with special educational needs (SEN) in their classrooms, with pupils who are exceptionally able, and in very small schools - all of these are circumstances in which the range of achievement is likely to be larger than average.

13   Teachers should provide regular mathematical activities and exercises for pupils to do at home, to extend their learning time for mathematics.

14   The TTA and DfEE should hold conferences to familiarise providers of INSET and ITT with the strategy, and consider its implications for trainee and serving teachers.

15   QCA's review of the National Curriculum should ensure that the Key Stage 1 and 2 mathematics curriculum has a greater emphasis on oral and mental calculation, and makes clear when formal written calculation methods are to be introduced, once these foundations are secure.

16   Calculators are best used in primary schools in the later years of Key Stage 2, and should not be used as a prop for simple arithmetic. Teachers should teach pupils how to use them constructively and efficiently. QCA's forthcoming guidance on mental calculation will help teachers to do this, and should complement the *Framework for teaching*.

17   Schools should involve classroom assistants, and other adult helpers, fully in the preparation for and implementation of the strategy. The DfEE should consider the scope for incorporating support for specialist teaching assistant (STA) training in at least the second year of the strategy.

18   The DfEE should invite bids from LEAs for pilot projects to support the development of numeracy skills at Key Stage 3.

19   Secondary heads of mathematics and teachers with responsibility for primary liaison should attend conferences about the strategy in the summer term 2000, to prepare for the first intake of 11 year olds to have experienced the National Numeracy Strategy.

20   The DfEE should begin planning in autumn 1998 for an educational slant to the UNESCO-led World Mathematical Year 2000, also with the aim of raising general public interest in mathematics.

21   Primary and special schools should set in hand arrangements to inform parents about the school's own approach to teaching mathematics and how the parents can help children to develop numeracy skills at home.

22   OFSTED should train its inspectors in the National Numeracy Strategy, and evaluate the effects of the strategy in a significant sample of schools.

23   TTA should ensure that its national professional standards for teachers and headteachers take into account their respective roles in supporting the numeracy strategy. It should also consider how best to use the World Mathematical Year 2000 to reinforce recruitment strategies for mathematics teachers.

24   The Basic Skills Agency should extend and develop its Family Numeracy pilot programme, taking into account in particular the need to ensure best value for money, and to link the activities closely to children's progress at school.

 # Consultation and the way ahead

Introduction

1 When the Task Force published its preliminary report, *Numeracy Matters*, in January of this year, we offered it for wide consultation to all those with an interest in mathematics education. This report builds on *Numeracy Matters*, offering our final recommendations to Ministers in the light of that consultation. It thus sets out a practical agenda for action for schools, LEAs and all others involved in implementing the National Numeracy Strategy.

2 We have been very pleased to find almost universal support for the broad philosophy and recommendations of *Numeracy Matters*, not least because we were aware that we were venturing into difficult territory. It appears that our preliminary report has not only made more people aware of the importance of mathematics, but also begun to crystallise agreement on measures that will raise standards for primary aged children. It is worth restating at the outset of this, our final report, the key beliefs that have guided the Task Force throughout its work, which we explained at the beginning of our preliminary report in January. These are as follows:

- **Looking at the evidence** We have aimed throughout our work to look at the evidence to find solutions to any problems with mathematics attainment, and to make practical recommendations based on methods that have been shown to be effective in raising standards of primary mathematics.

- **Building on existing best practice** Our overriding aim is to raise standards. We therefore wish to build on the best practice that is already happening in primary classrooms, rather than sweeping away the good along with what has been done less effectively.

- **The best of both worlds** We have attempted to learn not only from this country, but from achievements (and mistakes) in other countries, aiming for a blend of practice from this country and abroad that will improve standards in mathematics.

- **The importance of both home and school environments** We believe that children's families, as well as their schools, can help to raise their standards of achievement. Teachers and pupils need the support of parents and the wider community if they are to bring about the rise in children's mathematical attainment that we all wish to see.

- **Other developments in education** We have attempted to work with the grain of existing education policies, so as not to confuse or overload an already stretched primary teaching force. In particular, in framing this final report, which sets out how we believe the strategy should be implemented, we have sought to take on board the experience that teachers will already have of the National Literacy Strategy, and to learn from what has happened so far.

3   These beliefs are reflected in the ambitious programme we recommend to reach the government's national target for 2002, that is, for 75% of 11 year olds to reach Level 4 or better in the National Curriculum mathematics tests, the level expected for children of that age. We have also borne in mind throughout our work the important fact that this target is a staging post on the road to the ultimate target of virtually all 11 year olds achieving the standards of mathematics expected for their age by around 2007, and the few who do not do so also making appropriate progress. Our recommendations are therefore intended to benefit the 20 to 25 per cent of children who may not reach this standard in 2002, as well as those who will.

4   The National Numeracy Strategy is designed to affect every primary classroom, and special school classrooms with primary aged pupils, where teachers have a direct impact on pupils' achievements. It is also designed to influence the way in which schools, LEAs and national bodies manage the improvement of standards of numeracy, and every institution where primary teachers are trained, and to maximise the contribution that parents and the general community can make. The Task Force has also recognised that our work represents a part of a long term aim to improve the whole of mathematics education, at every level.

Responses to consultation

5 We undertook an extensive consultation process to test out the principles of our report and its detailed recommendations. Copies of the report were sent to all primary, secondary and special schools, initial teacher training providers, LEAs and organisations representing the interests of subject specialists, teachers, parents and businesses. Many copies were also sent out in response to requests from individuals. We held two consultation conferences, in London and Leeds, to which we invited every LEA to send three representatives, including at least one classroom teacher. These conferences gave members of the Task Force an invaluable opportunity to get direct, detailed feedback from the people who will have responsibility for implementing our final recommendations, and to discuss key issues. Members of the Task Force also spoke directly with many organisations concerned with mathematics and mathematics education. We are grateful to everyone who took the time and trouble to respond to our consultation, whether in writing or through their contributions to one of the conferences or other discussions.

6 Our preliminary report offered a number of "desired outcomes" that a National Numeracy Strategy should seek to bring about. There was no disagreement with these, nor with the principles governing how they should be achieved. In particular, there was agreement on the general principles that:

- the numeracy strategy should, where possible, follow the general structure of the National Literacy Strategy to decrease the potential for overload and build on the experience that teachers will have gained in implementing a major strategy for raising standards;

- available resources for training should be focused on the teachers who will need to make the strategy a reality day by day in the classroom; and

- the strategy should have an impact not only in schools and LEAs, but also on parents' role in helping children to acquire numeracy skills, and on the national perception of the importance of numeracy.

7   A wide range of organisations and individuals, whether practitioners, policy makers or researchers, agree with the Task Force about the blend of measures we put forward in our preliminary report as a means of raising standards. We were pleased to see in our consultation that people and organisations with different viewpoints now seem to be converging on a solid centre of agreed practice. This growing unity can only be for the good of mathematics as a subject, and for children and their teachers.

8   Our recommendations about the importance of oral and mental work, frequent high quality interaction with pupils - often in whole class settings - and regular timetabled mathematics lessons are all practices that are already being used in programmes such as the National Numeracy Project (NNP). Their importance is supported by inspection evidence and by the majority of research literature that we have been able to obtain. Many other countries are also aiming for this blend of practice. Some, for example, are seeking to continue with whole class instruction, with high quality interaction with pupils, but to add to it a greater focus on collaborative group work. These countries are also seeking to continue their relatively strong performance in number work, but to complement it with improved performance in the application of mathematics to real life contexts that this country has demonstrated.

9   Consultation responses revealed a number of concerns, however, about how the strategy could best be implemented so that our desired outcomes could be brought about. There were particular concerns about ensuring a sufficient training and support structure for schools to facilitate a national training exercise in a subject where teachers probably have less confidence than in literacy. There were also worries about ensuring that enough numeracy consultants were available to meet LEAs' needs, and about the level of continuing resources that would be needed to fund improvements. We recognise these concerns, and have taken them into account in framing our final recommendations.

What happens next?

10   *Numeracy Matters* explained, based on research and inspection evidence, the teaching methods and other factors that we believed would be effective in raising standards of numeracy in primary schools. This final report by the Task Force presents to Ministers firm recommendations about how these changes should be brought about. It thus constitutes a practical agenda for action, leading from the principles and desired outcomes of our preliminary report, and the responses to it. It will now be for the DfEE, in partnership with LEAs, schools, teachers, parents, higher education, OFSTED, QCA, TTA, and the Basic Skills Agency to make this agenda a reality, so that there will be a significant impact on the standards of numeracy attained by all pupils. In doing so, the DfEE will need to continue to ensure, with the help of its Literacy and Numeracy Strategy Group, that the two strategies together are coherent, and do not overburden schools.

11   The next chapter of this report sets out in some detail the training and support for schools that will lie at the heart of the strategy. This is followed by a chapter dealing with the strategies in schools, then by a chapter that sets out measures to create a climate of support for numeracy amongst parents and the wider community. At the end of each chapter there is a list of recommendations for action for the DfEE and other key agencies, schools and LEAs. These are set out term by term, to give an overview of how we see the strategy working from now - summer 1998 - onwards. All these recommendations are brought together in a summary, with a timetable for the strategy, at the end of this report. This autumn, we plan to publish a separate research report that will give useful background to the Task Force's work. This will consist of an annotated bibliography of the research material that has led us to the recommendations in *Numeracy Matters* and in this, our final report. Schools and all other interested parties will have the opportunity to order a copy. We hope that this will be of use and interest to all those - whether teachers, policy makers or researchers - who wish to explore in more detail the effective practice we have recommended.

The importance of numeracy

12   It is worth reiterating at the beginning of this final report that numeracy is an important life skill. This was reaffirmed in all the responses we received during consultation. We have all been greatly heartened by the profile that mathematics gained with the publication of *Numeracy Matters*. All those involved in implementing the strategy must now sustain this profile, and build on it as we carry forward the implementation of the National Numeracy Strategy into 1999/2000 and beyond. The recommendations in chapter 4, about creating a national climate of support for numeracy, will be especially important in this respect. There was also a wide welcome for our underlining the principle that all children have the right to become numerate, and our reminder that the ultimate aim of the strategy, beyond the 75% goal for 2002, was for virtually all children to reach the standard of mathematics expected for their age by 2007. Those who cannot, because they have particular special educational needs, should also have the opportunity through this strategy to improve their numeracy skills substantially.

13   There was a general consensus in consultation that the 2002 target, and ultimately, the more universal target, could be achieved. We asked in our preliminary report whether there should be some mechanism for publishing results to show progress of all children in a school towards the national target, not just those achieving at Level 4 and above. Those respondents who mentioned it supported this proposal, and tended to favour reporting of those reaching each level, rather than an average score. We are concerned, however, that any effort to show more comprehensive progress towards the target should not overload performance tables to a point at which they become unmanageable, and that giving such a level of detail should not publicly identify individual pupils. We therefore recommend that the DfEE should consult with LEAs on adding an average level for primary pupils at the end of Key Stage 2 to future performance tables. In this way, we hope that the progress of all children will become a more common currency when discussing progress towards targets, rather than simply the percentage of children at Level 4 and above. In addition, QCA should ensure that the mathematics tests for Key Stages 1 and 2 continue to provide a fair and consistent picture of national progress towards the 2002 target and beyond.

The definition of numeracy at primary level

14 A number of those responding to consultation said it would be helpful for the Task Force to make clear how numeracy relates to the broader area of mathematics. Numeracy is described below as a proficiency in various skills. The National Curriculum for mathematics at each level is in part focused directly upon such skills and in part upon laying the foundation for higher levels of mathematical study which, in turn, provide further skills valuable in adult life.

15 We have therefore developed the NNP definition of numeracy quoted in our preliminary report, and recommend that the following definition is used to underpin the National Numeracy Strategy:

"Numeracy at Key Stages 1 and 2 is a proficiency that involves a confidence and competence with numbers and measures. It requires an understanding of the number system, a repertoire of computational skills and an inclination and ability to solve number problems in a variety of contexts. Numeracy also demands practical understanding of the ways in which information is gathered by counting and measuring, and is presented in graphs, diagrams, charts and tables. This proficiency is promoted through giving a sharper focus to the relevant aspects of the National Curriculum programmes of study for mathematics.

Numerate primary pupils should be confident and competent enough to tackle problems without going immediately to teachers and friends for help. They should:

● have a sense of the size of a number and where it fits into the number system;

● know by heart number facts such as number bonds, multiplication tables, division facts, doubles and halves;

● use what they know by heart to figure out answers mentally;

● calculate accurately and efficiently, both mentally and on paper, drawing on a range of calculation strategies;

- recognise when it is appropriate to use a calculator - and when it is not - and be able to use one effectively;

- make sense of number problems, including non-routine problems, and recognise the operations needed to solve them;

- explain their methods and reasoning using correct mathematical terms;

- judge whether their answers are reasonable, and have strategies for checking them where necessary;

- suggest suitable units for measuring, and make sensible estimates of measurements; and

- explain and make predictions from the numbers in graphs, diagrams, charts and tables.

The National Numeracy Project

16 The teaching methods and training outlined in the Task Force's preliminary report were based in part on the National Numeracy Project (NNP), which has been running successfully since 1996. The preliminary report also showed that the NNP shares many key aims and methods of working with other projects begun at about that time, aimed at helping primary schools to teach the National Curriculum for mathematics in a way that raises standards of numeracy. These included the Barking and Dagenham Project, the Mathematics Enhancement Programme (Primary) and the Hamilton Maths Project.

17 It is evident from responses to consultation that the NNP enjoys wide support, and that many teachers are anxious to get copies of the *Framework for teaching* used by the teachers in the NNP, as soon as possible. There was a little concern that the Task Force should be quite sure of the effectiveness of NNP if a national strategy were to be based upon it. This concern is quite proper, but it is important to stress that the Task Force has been very impressed by the evident gains in pupils' achievements that the NNP has so far brought about in a wide range of schools. QCA has devised age standardised numeracy tests for schools participating in the NNP to show pupils' progress. The tests, which have mental and written components, are administered to pupils as their schools come into the project. Pupils' progress is measured by testing after a year and when the school leaves the project after two years. More than 23,000 pupils have already been tested and retested and the overall gains in their mean age standardised scores were significant. We are particularly encouraged that those who were achieving at the lowest level at the beginning of their school's involvement in the NNP were those who gained

most. We are also pleased that the NNP has proved effective with pupils with special educational needs.

18 We are aware that it will not be possible, within available financial and human resources, to give every primary and special school in the country exactly the same level of support that schools in the NNP have received. The Task Force has therefore sought to build on the aspects of the NNP support that schools find most valuable in changing their practice and raising standards, and also to ensure that schools most in need of a high level of support will receive it.

19 It is, of course, very important that the methods of the NNP continue to be subject to rigorous evaluation as they continue and are developed in the National Numeracy Strategy. It will be particularly important to investigate why some schools make more improvement than others, so that the strategy can be constantly developed and refined, particularly in terms of the help that is offered to schools in differing circumstances. The oversight of the evaluation is a key task for the DfEE's Literacy and Numeracy Strategy Group. Information about the relative effectiveness of different aspects of the strategies should be widely disseminated to LEAs and schools to encourage further positive development, and the government should, of course, further refine its policies in the light of this information.

Changes in the classroom

20 We recommend that from the autumn term 1999, a number of changes take place in the teaching of mathematics in primary classrooms, reflecting the teaching methods and other factors the Task Force considers to be effective, and set out in *Numeracy Matters*. These methods are already being implemented successfully in the NNP and other similar projects, and will, from September, underpin the initial training of primary teachers. We are pleased that the methods set out in our report enjoyed such wide support during consultation. The implementation of the strategy presents a unique opportunity to raise standards of mathematics for all children. We believe that all teachers will welcome the opportunity for training in effective mathematics teaching. We recognise and applaud the fact that some schools are already teaching mathematics successfully, and raising children's standards of attainment. The changes we recommend will mean a greater change in the classroom for some schools than others. Many schools reaching high standards of mathematics will already be using some or all of the methods we recommend. These and all other schools should be entitled to receive the training and support we recommend, which is set out in more detail in the next chapter.

21 It is worth reiterating first the key elements of practice that we recommended in *Numeracy Matters*, which have received widespread support in consultation, and which we recommend should be at the heart of the National Numeracy Strategy. Perhaps the most fundamental point in our preliminary report was the need to ensure that all children have regular sustained teaching of mathematics. We noted that whilst many schools gave quite a lot of time to the subject, the amount of mathematics teaching that individual children received could vary widely from class to class and pupil to pupil. We identified as a key objective for the strategy a daily mathematics lesson for all primary aged pupils, with good quality teaching. Our wish, therefore, is that by the autumn term 1999, all primary schools, and special schools with primary aged pupils, should provide a daily mathematics lesson of between 45 and 60 minutes for all their pupils, depending on their age. This also includes middle schools with primary aged pupils. A higher proportion of these lessons than before should focus on developing numeracy skills, and a much higher proportion of time than was previously the case in mathematics lessons should be spent teaching the whole class together. Our preliminary report also stressed the importance of frequent, well-directed oral and mental work to develop and reinforce pupils' calculation and recall skills. This, too, should feature strongly in the daily lessons.

22   We believe, as stated in *Numeracy Matters*, that every pupil should receive good direct teaching in the daily lesson that:

- gives them instruction and demonstrates, explains and illustrates mathematics, setting the work in different contexts and linking it to previous work;

- maximises the opportunities for the teacher to interact with pupils, so that they can talk and be listened to, and receive feedback that helps them to develop their mathematical knowledge, skills and understanding; and

- allows pupils to show what they know, explain their thinking and methods, and suggest alternative ways of tackling problems.

23   Direct teaching of the whole class together does not mean a return to the formal "chalk and talk" approach, with the teacher talking and pupils mainly just listening. Good direct teaching is lively and stimulating. It means that teachers provide clear instruction, use effective questioning techniques and make good use of pupils' responses. Teachers need to manage time in the lesson effectively so that pupils have time to think, practise individually and consolidate their knowledge, understanding and skills. It is important, too, that pupils spend some time working together in groups and in pairs, where they can, for example, collaborate in solving a problem, and keep their skills sharp through a variety of well paced activities, meeting individually set time targets or other challenges.

The *Framework for teaching*

24   Good planning is critical for the success of the daily mathematics lesson. The National Curriculum for mathematics sets out what pupils should be taught at each key stage.

Schools generally prepare their own schemes of work showing in detail how the curriculum will be covered, indicating what will be taught, how and when. The *Framework for teaching* is a key document that has been developed and used in the NNP. It is designed to help schools teach the National Curriculum by giving more detail of what should be taught. As noted above, numeracy should not be equated with mathematics. It is a proficiency that is acquired from being taught mathematics well, with a suitable emphasis on the parts of the curriculum that relate specifically to numeracy. The Framework gives teaching objectives that allow teachers to plan and teach the National Curriculum for mathematics in a way that develops pupils' numeracy skills to the full, using the methods that we have recommended as effective. The teaching objectives are set out year by year to allow teachers to plan and pace the work, and provide appropriate breadth and balance, so that pupils progress steadily in mathematics throughout their time in Key Stages 1 and 2.

25   The Task Force sees the Framework as an important practical tool for teachers in the National Numeracy Strategy. There was widespread support for the NNP's *Framework for teaching* in responses to consultation, and for our recommendation that it should be available to all primary teachers. Respondents were generally keen that all primary school teachers, and teachers in special schools, should be given a copy of the Framework soon, not least because many schools are already using it, and beginning to plan for implementing the National Numeracy Strategy. The Framework has been constantly reviewed and refined throughout the NNP, and it is important that teachers receive the final version as soon as practicable. It has already been further refined, drawing on the experience and expertise of a number of individuals drawn from the major mathematical associations. The DfEE should now facilitate further work on finalising the Framework, with input from QCA, OFSTED and TTA, and aim to send it to teachers in all schools as early as possible in 1999, also including it on the National Grid for Learning. Relevant QCA guidance documents, on mental calculation and exemplification of pupils' standards, should also be sent to schools at the same time. These are discussed in more detail in Chapter 3.

A universal strategy

26   The Task Force believes that the recommended strategy has something to offer every teacher and school. The training and support set out in the next chapter is a basic entitlement for all teachers in primary, middle and special schools. Teachers would all benefit from the extra knowledge of effective mathematics teaching, as part of their professional development. We also believe that providing this training for all teachers would help to offer continuity of experience for pupils within and between schools, where standards currently vary too much, and help the profession to develop a common language for speaking about good practice in mathematics teaching. As stated in *Numeracy Matters*, we believe that schools should also review their current practice and

understanding of mathematics using the *Framework for teaching*. In these senses, our recommended National Numeracy Strategy is a universal strategy. This is because all children have the same right to high standards. Some schools are already achieving well in difficult circumstances, and some are not doing well enough. Some schools are doing relatively well, but could improve their standards still further. The strategy should be able to meet the needs of all these schools. The ultimate target beyond 2002, of ensuring that virtually all 11 year olds reach the standard expected for their age by 2007, is, after all, likely to be demanding even for the schools that are currently most successful.

27   We therefore recommend that every primary and special school should participate in the basic training for all schools. Primary schools, and, where appropriate, special schools, should use the practices that we have identified as effective ways of raising standards of mathematics, by:

> ● reviewing, and adjusting where necessary, their planning and teaching practices in mathematics, using the *Framework for teaching* as a tool to help them do so;
>
> ● teaching all their pupils a daily 45 to 60 minute mathematics lesson;
>
> ● teaching mathematics to all pupils within a class at the same time, with a high proportion of lessons concentrating on the development of numeracy skills;
>
> ● teaching mathematics to the whole class or to groups for a high proportion of the lesson, promoting participation from, and co-operation between, pupils;
>
> ● including oral and mental work within each daily mathematics lesson; and
>
> ● providing regular mathematical activities and exercises that pupils can do at home.

28   The *Framework for teaching* gives guidance on meeting the National Curriculum requirements for mathematics in ways that promote children's numeracy skills. It is therefore non-statutory, but has received a good deal of support in consultation. The Task Force believes that all schools will find the Framework a valuable tool for reviewing and adjusting their practice in mathematics, and that many will wish to use it for planning their daily mathematics lesson. There is, after all, no sense in teachers inventing many different solutions to problems and challenges that are common to all. It is important, however, that schools should make a professional judgement, once they have reviewed their current practice using the Framework, and in the light of the training, about the degree to which they will need to adjust their current practices and follow the Framework in detail.

29   As recommended in our preliminary report, we believe that schools should take the decision about how they use the training in consultation with their LEA and the appropriate Regional Director for the strategy. The following factors should influence the extent to which a school changes its current practices:

> - pupils' past, current and expected attainment in mathematics - is a school likely to meet its target for improvement?;
>
> - the quality of the teaching in the school and how it compares with the practices identified within the strategy as effective - does the school teach a daily mathematics lesson to all pupils and use the time effectively?;
>
> - the quality of a school's planning and monitoring of its teaching - how do the teaching objectives and expectations of pupils compare with the level and rigour of those in the Framework?;
>
> - the efficiency of the school's management procedures - is it effective in evaluating its strengths and weaknesses in mathematics, and in planning further action to maintain or improve standards?;
>
> - the curriculum leadership within the school - can the school sustain improvements in teaching and standards of achievement, with strong support from senior management?;
>
> - whether the school is already involved in a good quality, properly supported programme to raise standards in primary mathematics - we believe that the schools involved in the projects mentioned in *Numeracy Matters* (the Barking and Dagenham project, the Hamilton Maths Project and the Mathematics Enhancement Programme) will already be using many of the practices we have identified as effective, making it possible both to participate in the national strategy and to continue their own project development.

30   There will be considerable variation amongst schools in the extent to which they are currently using the practices that we have recommended as effective, and thus, the extent to which they will need to make changes in the classroom. It is conceivable that there are schools already achieving very good results, both in terms of achievement in national tests and in comparison to schools in similar circumstances, using only some of the methods we have recommended, or perhaps even none at all. Even in these cases, we consider it is important for the school to participate in the national training and then to consider their own practice. In every case, the effect of a school's action, in the light of the strategy, on children's achievement in mathematics should be the most important consideration of all.

The structure of the daily lesson

31   The structure of the daily mathematics lessons in primary and, where appropriate, special schools, should be based on the structure used successfully in the NNP. This structure uses the teaching methods we have identified as effective. The length of the lesson should vary according to the ages of the children involved. It should last for about 45 minutes for children in Key Stage 1 in Years 1 and 2, 50 minutes in Years 3 and 4 and increase to 1 hour in Years 5 and 6, with some flexibility in length for special schools. The structure of the daily lesson in the NNP emphasises the need for daily oral and mental work, in line with the recommendations in our preliminary report, where we stated that children should be secure with the foundations of numeracy before they are introduced to formal written methods. We also said that it was important for pupils to practise and strengthen their mental recall and calculation skills throughout primary school.

32   The implications of teaching this daily lesson are discussed in more detail in chapter 3, but it is probably helpful to set out at the beginning of this report how we expect a typical lesson in the numeracy strategy to work:

Clear Start to Lesson		
Whole class	• mental and oral work to rehearse and sharpen skills	About 5 to 10 minutes
Main Teaching and Pupil Activities		
Whole class/Groups/ Pairs/Individuals	• clear objectives shared with pupils • interactive/direct teaching input • pupils clear about what to do next • practical and/or written work on the same theme for all the class • if group work, usually differentiated at no more than 3 levels of difficulty, with focused teaching of 1 or 2 groups for part of the time • continued interaction and intervention • misconceptions identified	About 30 to 40 minutes
Plenary		
Whole class	• feedback from children to identify progress and sort misconceptions • summary of key ideas, what to remember • links made to other work, next steps discussed • work set to do at home	About 10 to 15 minutes

33   This outline structure should not be seen as a mechanistic recipe to be followed. Teachers should use their professional judgement to determine the activities, timing and organisation in each part of the lesson to suit their teaching objectives. In the main part of the lesson, in particular, there would be a different mix of work with the whole class, groups, pairs and individuals on different days. But each lesson should also include some direct teaching and interaction with the pupils, and activities or exercises that pupils do themselves. Overall, there should be a high proportion of work with the whole class, but there may be more in some lessons - for example, those at the start of a new topic - than in others.

OFSTED

34   We stated in *Numeracy Matters* that OFSTED should take the strategy into account in inspections of schools and LEAs, and should ensure that inspectors were well prepared to inspect numeracy and informed about the National Numeracy Strategy. They should also have a key role in helping the DfEE to evaluate the impact of the strategy.

35   HMI have been inspecting schools participating in the NNP, reporting their findings to the DfEE and the Project Director. They will continue to carry out this evaluation. OFSTED has already begun an inspection programme to evaluate the impact of the National Literacy Strategy, and plans to carry out a similar programme for the numeracy strategy. On the basis of the recommendations in the next chapter, this programme will include visits to LEAs to inspect the training of co-ordinators and teachers, the management of the strategy and its impact on particular schools. In line with the recommendation in our preliminary report, inspectors will also make visits to a structured sample of nearly 300 schools throughout the strategy, a significant proportion of which will be receiving more intensive support.

36   Regular inspections of schools will also give information about the impact of the strategy on standards of mathematics. It is important that OFSTED ensures that all inspectors are trained to inspect numeracy in schools, in advance of the beginning of the strategy in autumn 1999. Inspectors should understand what they are to inspect in the numeracy strategy, and how to go about it. This training should take account of the materials used in the national training programmes for headteachers, mathematics co-ordinators and teachers.

 # Training and support for schools

Introduction

37 In *Numeracy Matters*, the Task Force set out the methods of teaching that we believed, on consideration of the research and inspection evidence, and on the experience of projects like the NNP, would be most effective in raising standards. Those responding to consultation have expressed virtually no disagreement with the key aspects of these methods. The Task Force must now make proposals about how best to provide the training and other support that will equip teachers and schools to put these methods into practice, to enhance their professional skills and raise standards. Many responses to consultation mentioned concerns about the need to increase teachers' subject knowledge and confidence in mathematics. The training we envisage for all schools, and the distribution of the *Framework for teaching* and other materials, will begin to address this problem. We also see the enhancement of subject knowledge as a priority for teachers' continuing professional development within and beyond the strategy.

Overall structure of training and support

38   It is clear from responses to consultation that LEAs and schools do not want the structure and implementation of the National Numeracy Strategy to be different from the National Literacy Strategy just for the sake of being different. Schools are now familiar with the literacy strategy, and geared up to take part in, and act on, the training and other support. At the same time, the Task Force has not been afraid to modify this structure where schools can be perceived to have different needs in numeracy, or where lessons can be learnt from the implementation of the literacy strategy. We aim to make the strategy easy for schools and LEAs to implement, with a programme of professional development that has a real impact on standards and obtains the best value for money from the government funding that is likely to be available.

39   Those responding to consultation felt strongly that schools should receive a high degree of direct support, with the whole staff of a school being trained together wherever possible. The Task Force agrees that external support is desirable for all schools, but recognises that it is particularly important where the school is relatively weak in mathematics, and the mathematics co-ordinator may be less well equipped to lead professional development than in other schools. It appears from our consultation that schools are more keenly aware of a need for direct support in numeracy than they are in literacy, because primary teachers tend to have less confidence about their teaching skills and subject knowledge in this area. This does not mean, of course, that teachers do not also need subject knowledge training in literacy. It does suggest, however, that it will be very important to boost teachers' confidence early on in the National Numeracy Strategy, so that they believe from the outset that changes can be achieved.

40   We have borne in mind that information and training need to be available for every primary teacher and special school teacher at the earliest possible stage. At the same time, however, both the Task Force and those responding to consultation recognise that it is the headteacher and mathematics co-ordinator who need specific training in order to lead the changes within a school. It is also important to remember that, like the National Literacy Strategy, the numeracy strategy is huge in its ambition and scope. A professional development programme of this size cannot easily provide whole school training for all teachers on the scale of, say, the NNP. Some schools, but not all, will need intensive support that comes close to this. Some schools will already be doing well, and will have realistic plans for achieving their targets. These will mainly need to familiarise themselves with the Framework, amend their existing schemes of work and teaching styles as appropriate, and undertake the basic training. For the strategy to have maximum effect, every school will also need to build on the foundations of this professional development in future years.

Funding

41   The National Literacy Strategy has received around £50 million of funding from the Standards Fund in 1998-99. Funding for the strategy is expected to remain at about that level up to 2002, and we expect that a similar amount will be available for the National Numeracy Strategy from 1999-2000. The Task Force has taken the experience from the NNP into account in order to ensure that our recommendations focus resources on the elements of training that appear to be most important for building up teachers' knowledge and skills, and their confidence and effectiveness in the classroom. We have taken into account the likely funding parameters and the comments received during consultation, in order to make recommendations that we think will secure an optimum level of support for all schools.

42   The Standards Fund allocation for the National Literacy Strategy in 1998-99, excluding the allocation for schools already in the NLP, was split roughly as follows:

LEA consultants and administrative support	£10.3m
Supply cover for schools	£12.8m
Books for schools	£19.0m
Key Stage 3 programmes	£ 3.2m
Specialist Teaching Assistants (STA) training	£ 2.3m

43   Our recommendations replicate key parts of this expenditure for the numeracy strategy, but there are some differences. The main variation is that we do not recommend a specific allocation of expenditure for books and other resources for schools to support mathematics. Classroom resources are discussed in more detail in the next chapter. We see the provision of opportunities for teachers to observe good practice and receive other training as the most important priority in the first year of the strategy, and have therefore sought to maximise such opportunities within the funds available. A breakdown of our estimated costs is set out in Annex I of this report. We recognise, however, that the overall size and distribution of the Standards Fund grant will be for Ministers to determine.

Observing successful teaching

44   It is clear from the experience of the NNP that a crucial element of training, which makes individual teachers realise that they can make changes happen in their own classrooms, is the opportunity to see someone else teach a successful mathematics lesson based on the Framework. Responses to consultation indicate that teachers would greatly value these opportunities as part of the National Numeracy Strategy, and we have sought to make them as widely available as possible within the likely funding.

45   We believe that all primary and special school teachers should have at least one opportunity to observe a successful mathematics lesson that reflects the principles of the National Numeracy Strategy, as early on in the strategy as possible. This opportunity could be provided in different ways, depending on the level of a school's needs. Teachers should watch at least one of the following:

- an **LEA numeracy consultant** teach one or more lessons in the teacher's own school, a nearby school, or in a demonstration session given, for example, as part of an INSET day;

- a local **"leading mathematics teacher"**, nominated by the LEA, teaching their own class in their own school or, less commonly, in another school;

- the **mathematics co-ordinator** or another colleague in the teacher's own school teaching either their own or the teacher's class; and

- lessons taught on the **video training material** to be sent to all schools as a key part of the strategy.

46   Our recommended strategy would provide for all of these opportunities, but the type and extent of the opportunities offered would need to be determined locally, depending on each school's needs. In every case, teachers should also take time to reflect on and discuss what they had seen and how it related to their own work in the classroom.

47   The next four sections of this chapter look in more detail at each of these options for providing demonstration lessons, and the role in the strategy for LEA numeracy consultants, local "leading mathematics teachers", and mathematics co-ordinators.

LEA numeracy consultants

The role of consultants

48   There was strong support in responses to consultation for the idea of numeracy consultants working in a similar way to the more than 200 literacy consultants now recruited to offer direct support to schools as they implement the National Literacy Strategy. The role of numeracy consultants within the NNP is to help schools audit their own performance and their training and other needs, and to provide direct training and support for teachers, including twilight sessions. They also help schools to develop their

whole school policies for mathematics and carry forward the new approach to mathematics into their day to day teaching. A key part of an NNP consultant's job is teaching demonstration lessons in the schools he or she is supporting. The experience of the NNP is that regular support from consultants is crucial in building up teachers' confidence and effectiveness as they make changes in teaching methods and seek to raise standards of achievement in their schools. We believe that numeracy consultants should play a key role in the National Numeracy Strategy.

Recruitment of consultants

49 Those responding to consultation recognised that the availability of good quality numeracy consultants would be crucial to the success of the National Numeracy Strategy. The consensus appears to be that the need for this support is, if anything, greater than in the literacy strategy, though the experience of the NNP suggests that some LEAs might find it hard to recruit enough suitable consultants. The consultants should have recent practical experience of teaching in the primary classroom. This, and a salary level of around £30,000, suggests that the prime recruitment field for consultants would be experienced primary or special school teachers. There is understandable concern that recruitment of consultants could remove the best mathematics co-ordinators and other experienced teachers from primary and special school classrooms, and that schools might not have time to fill the gaps before the strategy begins. The Task Force recognises and shares these concerns, which the DfEE has now explored further. A sample of LEAs and schools, both inside and outside the NNP, were asked more detailed questions about the need for support in schools to improve standards of numeracy, and the most effective means of providing it. This has given the Task Force additional information to supplement the responses to consultation, which is reflected in this chapter.

50 It is difficult to gauge accurately whether the feeling in schools that more support is needed for numeracy than literacy is a true reflection of teachers' mathematical and pedagogical competence, as well as of their confidence. Both clearly have an impact on teachers' effectiveness in the classroom, and need support to be developed further. Each consultant in the NNP typically supports twenty schools in a year. Replicating this nationally would imply around 1,000 consultants, which clearly exceeds the resources available, even if suitably qualified individuals could be found. We believe it is most important that consultants focus their main efforts on those schools that are weakest in mathematics. These are the schools that will need sustained support if standards are to improve right across the country. Schools that do not fall into this category can receive other kinds of support, especially at the outset of the strategy, that boosts their confidence and competence relatively quickly, with some receiving a limited amount of continuing support from the consultant. A fairly modest increase in the number of numeracy consultants, of up to 100 more than the number funded through the Standards Fund for the literacy strategy, would nonetheless be possible. Any more than this would be in danger of eroding the funding likely to be available for supply cover for training and for release time to allow teachers to view demonstration lessons and work with mathematics co-ordinators and other colleagues.

Training and support for consultants

51 Prospective consultants will not emerge from the classroom instantly equipped to fulfil their new roles. The training for NNP consultants appears to have been generally highly effective in giving them a good knowledge of the Framework and the ability to impart that knowledge to others in a way that will allow teachers to take practical steps to change their own practice. In the course of implementing the strategy, however, consultants will encounter wider issues requiring skills that cannot necessarily be developed in the classroom, or in their initial training. In some schools, for example, an important part of the consultant's role will be to work to gain the support and commitment of a school's leadership to implement change. This might be difficult for a specialist numeracy consultant, who was until recently a classroom teacher. It is therefore important that consultants are supported by the LEA, as well as the regional management structure provided by the DfEE to manage the National Numeracy Strategy. LEA advisory staff should offer assistance in dealing with these situations to ensure that the strategy remains on course, and that the numeracy consultant is able to carry out his or her role effectively.

52 We believe that it is important to identify the people who will appointed as numeracy consultants early enough for them to receive locally-based training from the strategy's Regional Directors. We would expect numeracy consultants to be employed by LEAs on the same terms as literacy consultants, that is, a three year contract. If LEAs could be told in September the numbers of numeracy consultants the DfEE will be prepared to fund, they could place advertisements and recruit by Christmas 1998 for personnel to take up post at the beginning of April 1999. This timing would also allow schools more time to plan for replacing staff who leave at the end of the spring term. We hope that the DfEE could provide funding in 1998-99 to allow the consultants' existing employers to release them for up to ten days of initial training during the spring term 1999, so that they begin on 1 April properly prepared for their challenging roles. It is also important that consultants receive continuing training and support from the DfEE and their Regional Directors as the strategy proceeds.

Local "leading mathematics teachers"

The role of "leading mathematics teachers"

53 The Task Force believes that there will be strong demand for demonstration lessons, especially at the beginning of the strategy, when teachers may be uncertain about exactly what whole class teaching in mathematics will require of them. The consultants will not be able to meet all of this early demand on their own. We therefore propose that there should be local teachers in every LEA who supplement the numeracy consultants' input by acting as "leading mathematics teachers". We believe that skilled mathematics co-ordinators and teachers who have a particular strength in teaching mathematics could play a very valuable role in supporting and encouraging colleagues in other schools at this point of high demand at the very beginning of the strategy. Whilst we see this as their main input, we hope that these "leading mathematics teachers" would also be prepared to continue to act in a supportive role when the strategy is under way.

54   The main purpose of these leading teachers should be to offer other teachers the opportunity to see successful teaching based on the *Framework for teaching*, supplementing the opportunities for demonstration lessons offered by the consultants. This recommendation reflects the principle of the Beacon Schools initiative, but is much more specific in that it would focus on mathematics only, and on individual teachers rather than a whole school. In most cases, these teachers would teach demonstration lessons in their own schools in the first year of the strategy, and teachers from nearby schools would watch the lessons using release time provided for all schools. This would minimise the disruption to the schools of the "leading mathematics teachers", as the teachers would largely remain with their own classes, with some time for feedback and discussion. It would also be possible for leading teachers to visit other schools to teach demonstration lessons in those schools, but we would expect this approach to be used less frequently.

55   The expertise of these teachers would not only be crucial for their own school's success in implementing the strategy, but also benefit other schools. We are confident that teachers who have already enjoyed success in teaching mathematics - whether their school as a whole is doing well in mathematics, or whether they are one teacher with particular expertise within a school - would be prepared to take up this challenge. The main input would be concentrated at the beginning of the strategy, and we are convinced that this would offer an excellent opportunity for the teachers concerned to enhance their professionalism and personal development, and offer them and their school as a whole opportunities to forge closer links with colleagues in other local schools.

Identifying and training "leading mathematics teachers"

56   We envisage that LEAs would invite schools to identify particular co-ordinators or other teachers who have particular strength in teaching mathematics and who would be able to provide these demonstration lessons. The most important factor is the quality of the individual teacher, although in most cases the school as a whole should have good results in mathematics in comparison with schools in similar circumstances, or have

made substantial and rapid improvements. We expect that the individual teachers might have taken part in the 5 to 20 day mathematics subject knowledge courses previously funded through the Grants for Education Support and Training (GEST). They might also be ITT mentors who have been preparing with their partner HEIs, during the past year, to deliver and assess the new ITT National Curriculum for primary mathematics. It would obviously be desirable for the teachers to be identified early, around the same time as the consultants. The numbers of these teachers needed will vary between LEAs. It will depend on the size of the LEA, the needs of the schools and the number of consultants the LEA will recruit. We would estimate a typical ratio of around five "leading mathematics teachers" to one consultant. The DfEE should provide LEAs with guidance to help them, in consultation with schools, to identify these teachers, and subsequently facilitate arrangements for utilising them. These teachers would also need to receive up to five days of training in the spring term 1999, led by LEAs and assisted by Regional Directors. This would demand some extra DfEE funding for supply cover in 1998-99. The training should focus on the Framework, and the skills involved in teaching demonstration lessons and helping others to benefit from watching them.

School clusters

57   The Task Force is very much in favour of using school cluster arrangements as a means of spreading good practice in a local area, and of enabling teachers to encourage each other and build up the necessary confidence to make changes in their individual practice. Clusters are a particularly good support mechanism for mathematics co-ordinators. In any one area, there are likely to be schools with experienced and confident co-ordinators, and others where co-ordinators are newly appointed and less sure about their role. Regular meetings of co-ordinators in these clusters, to share ideas, experiences and common solutions to common problems, will help to get the strategy off to a good start and sustain progress thereafter. The ideal situation would be for a cluster to be built around one or two schools with a "leading mathematics teacher", so that teachers can establish a relationship with those teachers, and with each other as they learn from them. Special schools should be included in these clusters, whether with mainstream schools, or in a network of their own.

58   Many LEAs will, of course, have existing clusters in their areas. We do not propose that LEAs build up clusters specifically for the National Numeracy Strategy - the strategy will be built on strong foundations, and better sustained, if it uses existing clusters and other local networks of schools. Where these do not already exist, however, LEAs should immediately begin to encourage schools to group together in this way. We believe that cluster arrangements can be used to encourage improvements and collaboration in virtually every area of a school's work, including, of course, literacy.

Mathematics co-ordinators in all primary and middle schools, and in special schools with primary aged pupils

59 The emphasis on the role of mathematics co-ordinators in the Task Force's preliminary report, and on the importance of ensuring that they have the time and skills to fulfil their role effectively, was widely welcomed in responses to consultation, albeit with some concern that the amount of time for them to do this suggested in the report might not be enough. Our proposals for identifying "leading mathematics teachers" to supplement the LEA numeracy consultants further underlines the importance of this type of support. Over time, however, it should be not only these leading teachers, but mathematics co-ordinators in every primary and special school who teach demonstration lessons and help their colleagues to improve their own classroom practice. The headteacher in each school should drive the changes, by providing the necessary leadership and support within the school, ensuring that this is translated into action in the classroom, and driving improvements in teaching throughout the strategy and beyond. We see the mathematics co-ordinator in each primary and special school as the person who would provide major support for the headteacher in effecting the implementation of the changes we want to bring about. It is, of course, important that mathematics co-ordinators themselves receive training in order to do this, to make them familiar with the National Numeracy Strategy, and able to disseminate information and good practice to their colleagues. Some co-ordinators would find this easier than others. By definition, the most effective co-ordinators would already have been identified as "leading mathematics teachers", and would therefore be helping not only their own colleagues, but teachers from other local schools. In many cases, their schools would be achieving relatively high standards in mathematics.

60 Our priority for all other co-ordinators must be to equip them as quickly as possible to establish the daily mathematics lesson in their own classroom, and to lead INSET for their colleagues based on the national distance learning materials to be provided. Our recommendations envisage that the schools most in need of help would have the support of a numeracy consultant to help the co-ordinator do this. Some co-ordinators would be able to offer effective demonstration lessons and other support to colleagues fairly soon in the strategy, and we certainly hope that virtually all would be able to do so by the summer term 2000. This type of support is an important way of helping teachers to continue to improve their practice, and funding for in-school release time for this purpose should be maintained throughout the strategy. Thus, whilst at the beginning of the strategy, teachers would be more likely to be watching a lesson taught by a consultant or a "leading mathematics teacher", we expect that, later on, they would be more likely to be watching demonstration lessons taught by their own co-ordinator. The Task Force believes that as much release time as possible for watching demonstration lessons and supporting colleagues should be funded within the Standards Fund. There would, however, need to be some flexibility for LEAs to use the funding according to individual schools' needs, whether because of the standards they have already achieved, or their relative size. Schools themselves should also make the provision of release time a priority.

Video training material

61   The Task Force believes that good quality material on video has a vital role to play in the successful implementation of the National Numeracy Strategy. All schools should have access to nationally produced, high quality distance learning materials that can be used for training during INSET days at the school, as with the National Literacy Strategy. Further details of what this training should cover are given below. One of the most important advantages of including video material with this training is that it would give every primary, middle and special school teacher in the country an opportunity to see successful, whole class mathematics teaching reflecting the good practice we have identified, at the beginning of the strategy. This would be especially useful for illustrating, for example, effective instruction and interaction with the whole class or using different types of questioning, and for showing teachers implementing the lesson structure with a variety of pupils. Watching the video should leave teachers feeling more confident about using this highly effective form of mathematics teaching from the autumn term 1999.

62   Some teachers, especially those in the schools most in need of help with mathematics, should get to see a "live" demonstration lesson at an early stage of the strategy. The video material would supplement their experience, allowing the teachers to view the lesson in parts, to look at some parts several times, and discuss it with colleagues. The video material should also be used as a permanent resource that teachers can revisit throughout the strategy, either individually or at group training sessions. For those teachers who do not have an immediate opportunity to watch a "live" lesson, the video would obviously be especially valuable. The Task Force envisages that more than one video should be provided at the start of the strategy - a basic video of one or more successful mathematics lessons, followed by others looking at specific teaching methods within the lesson, and the teaching of specific topics, in more detail.

63   The DfEE should begin to prepare these new videos as soon as possible, to ensure that they are of the highest quality and are relevant and accessible for teachers. They would need to be available to schools by the summer term 1999 at the latest. There are several existing videos produced by the NNP, Hamilton Maths Project, OFSTED and the Barking and Dagenham Project. These could be used as a starting point for reviewing the most effective ways of presenting materials on mathematics teaching, but the strategy videos should be made up of new material. This exemplification of teaching practice on video should be an ongoing process, making the most of the opportunities that exist to include information about effective mathematics teaching. Practical teaching examples should also be offered to teachers on the National Grid for Learning and on CD Rom. The video material should show successful mathematics teaching in a variety of realistic situations, including small schools, pupils with English as an additional language (EAL) or SEN in mainstream classrooms, and special schools.

64   We are very aware that schools will begin to implement the National Numeracy Strategy at the end of the year in which they will have been heavily involved in the National Literacy Strategy. The literacy strategy will give schools valuable experience of implementing a whole school strategy to raise standards. Although we recognise that it will be quite demanding to implement the numeracy strategy immediately afterwards, we believe that schools will be able to build on the momentum, knowledge and experience that the literacy strategy will have given them. It will be important for the videos, and other distance learning material produced as part of the National Numeracy Strategy, to take this into account, and complement the materials produced for the literacy strategy. By autumn 1999, teachers will have been trained in a range of skills for the classroom, such as active teaching of the whole class in the literacy hour, which will be essential in numeracy and literacy alike. Some topics, including effective teaching of mathematics, familiarity with the *Framework for teaching*, and the detailed structure of the daily mathematics lesson, will be new, but others may only need some recapitulation.

The training programme for all schools

Leadership and management - headteachers, mathematics co-ordinators and governors

65   Teachers responding to the consultation were generally anxious to be trained as quickly as possible. There was a strong feeling that training of classroom teachers was the most important element of the strategy. Yet it was also acknowledged that change cannot happen unless it is driven by the headteacher. Where schools have been most successful in the NNP, it is clear that the commitment and clear leadership of the headteacher was a key contributory factor. The Task Force therefore believes that there should be training for the headteacher at the outset so that a clear agenda is set for change and that there should be training for classroom teachers as quickly as possible thereafter so that teachers can move in the direction the headteacher will set. We believe that the mathematics co-ordinator and an additional teacher from each primary and special school should also attend this initial training, as a means of building up teachers' confidence quickly at the start of the strategy. In most primary schools, and particularly those with a high proportion of pupils on the special needs register, we hope that this additional teacher would be the SENCO.

66 It is the headteacher who will take overall responsibility for auditing the school's needs at the outset of the strategy, identifying current standards of mathematics across the school, and the strengths and weaknesses in mathematics teaching, and deciding, in consultation with the LFA, how the school can best make the most of the training and materials that will be provided in the strategy. The materials sent to all schools will include detailed advice on how to carry out this audit. It is a key part of the process of securing improvements in mathematics, and LEAs should provide advice and support to headteachers as they take this forward. They will be used to carrying out audits of strengths and weaknesses through school development plans, the new requirements for school target setting, and the audit they will have carried out for the National Literacy Strategy. The training will need to take all this experience into account, and ensure that the audit for the National Numeracy Strategy builds on these different processes, and is consistent with them. National benchmarks of pupil performance and OFSTED's Performance and Assessment Reports (PANDAs), and for special schools locally developed benchmark data, are all important tools to help schools have a clear view of how their performance in literacy and numeracy compares with other, similar schools. Schools may also find it helpful to use a tool like the Basic Skills Agency's Quality Mark for Primary Schools, which has literacy and numeracy as its major focus, and may help them plan improvements in both areas in a way that achieves coherence and appropriate prominence for both.

67 The governing body of a school shares responsibility with the headteacher for raising standards, a fact recognised in the National Literacy Strategy by the involvement of a governor in the two day conference on the management of literacy. It is evident from consultation on our preliminary report that there is a desire for training in numeracy to be directed mainly at those who will make a direct impact in the classroom, namely the teachers, with training for governors targeted on the aspects of the strategy that will most directly concern them. It is important for governors to have a grasp of the National Numeracy Strategy, and key issues relating to managing it at school level, some of which will be common to both strategies. We do not expect, therefore, that a representative of the governing body will need training for more than one day, jointly with the headteacher, mathematics co-ordinator and other teacher, in order to do this.

68 This first training course should be attended by three members of staff from every primary and special school, plus one governor for the third day. It should prepare these key people for the management of the strategy within each school, and prepare the headteacher, supported by the mathematics co-ordinator, to lead whole school INSET. The course should not repeat aspects of the National Literacy Strategy that will have given schools general preparation, such as the generic skills of carrying out an audit of the school's strengths and weaknesses in a subject, target setting, and a whole school approach to involving parents, but it is important to note in planning course content that the mathematics co-ordinator and maybe the SENCO are unlikely to have attended the comparable three day course for the literacy strategy in 1998.

69 With all this in mind, the Task Force considers that the course should cover:

Day 1

- an overview of the classroom and school-based elements of the National Numeracy Strategy, including the *Framework for teaching;*

- the structure of the daily mathematics lesson;

- effective teaching; and

- approaches to calculation.

Day 2

- developing medium term teaching plans, using the Framework; and

- working with pupils with particular needs (e.g. SEN, EAL and able pupils).

70 Some special schools, such as those catering for pupils with severe learning difficulties or particular disabilities, should have the opportunity to use this second day to cover issues of particular relevance to them. The other two days should be equally relevant to all schools.

71 Day 3 (a governor also attends, having received a written overview of the strategy in advance for familiarisation).

- auditing and monitoring mathematics, concentrating on the subject specific issues of the evaluation of the planning, teaching and standards of mathematics, with only a little on target setting and action planning, which will have been covered in the National Literacy Strategy;

- implementing and sustaining change; and

- preparing to teach demonstration lessons.

72 For aspiring headteachers, the NPQH should ensure familiarity with the strategy, and emphasise the importance of the headteacher's role.

Whole school INSET

73   We have already made clear in this chapter that we see the provision of high quality examples of successful mathematics teaching as probably the most essential ingredient for making the National Numeracy Strategy work. As noted above, we believe that every teacher in every school should have access to nationally produced distance learning material, especially video material, which will be used in their school over three INSET days.

74   The first INSET day is the prime opportunity for uniting all the teachers in a primary, middle or special school behind the improvements in mathematics standards and changes in practice that the National Numeracy Strategy will entail. It should take place towards the end of the summer term 1999, after the headteacher and co-ordinator have attended their initial training course. Its purpose is to equip all the other teachers to begin implementing the daily mathematics lesson at the start of the autumn term 1999. It should therefore give teachers oversight of:

- the National Numeracy Strategy;

- the use of the *Framework for teaching* to plan the structure of the daily mathematics lesson, ensuring that the structure is fit for the purpose of the lesson;

- the characteristics of good teaching, including effective questioning techniques; and

- effective use of the beginnings and ends of the lesson.

75   It will be important for the schools identified as needing more intensive support than others to have some input from the consultant at an early stage. The Task Force believes that it would be valuable for the whole staff of these schools to come together with other schools for this first INSET day. The INSET days would probably need to be staggered within some LEAs, to allow two or three such sessions to be run, with 100 participants as an absolute maximum, and fewer where possible. The consultant would lead the training using the national distance learning materials, and answer direct questions from teachers. This kind of direct input from the consultant at an early stage may prove to be a crucial factor in encouraging teachers in the schools most in need of support to take the strategy on board and change practice in their own classrooms. Schools that are not identified by the LEA as needing intensive support may also find it useful to join together for this first INSET day, which could be led by one or more "leading mathematics teachers" within a local cluster of schools, and could also include a demonstration lesson.

76   The next two INSET days should further develop the skills and knowledge necessary to teach the daily mathematics lesson. The second INSET day should be at the beginning of the autumn term 1999, and cover:

- approaches to calculation, mental and written;

- the teaching and recording of mental calculation methods;

- the effective use of key classroom resources such as number lines; and

- teaching number facts and multiplication tables in enjoyable and varied ways.

77   The next INSET day should be in the spring term 2000, covering:

- progression from mental methods to the teaching of written calculation methods; and

- assessment, including identifying and correcting pupils' errors and misconceptions, and target setting for individual pupils.

78   This cumulative training should allow all classroom teachers gradually to improve and refine their practice, so that by around the middle of the autumn term 1999, they are all implementing the daily mathematics lesson in detail. The training should equip them, as their knowledge and confidence increases, to provide the daily lesson with growing effectiveness throughout the school year 1999/2000, using opportunities to observe other lessons, whether taught by a local "leading mathematics teacher" or their own mathematics co-ordinator, as additional development opportunities.

Support from consultants to meet schools' different needs

Schools needing intensive support

79   As already noted, the Task Force believes that the numeracy consultants should give priority to supporting schools in the greatest need of intensive support, as in the National Literacy Strategy. We expect that many of these schools will be in the lowest 10 to 15 per cent of mathematics attainment nationally in National Curriculum tests, but recommend that this is measured over at least two years to gain a consistent and balanced picture of schools' needs relative to one another, and take account of the progress schools have made over a period of time. It may be that some schools with results at higher national levels nonetheless need a good deal of support to bring their performance up to the level of similar schools around them. As in the National Literacy Strategy, it would be important for LEAs to decide how and when this support should be targeted during the three years of the strategy to 2002. By the time the strategy is implemented, they will also have access to value-added data to help them make these decisions. Some schools might need to continue with quite intensive support for more than one year - perhaps even the full three years of the strategy, up to 2002, which is even more than schools in the NNP receive. It is also important to recognise that many of the schools in need of intensive support for literacy are also likely to need it for numeracy. LEAs should ensure that the support is planned in a way that makes it manageable for schools, consulting with schools when deciding how the best use can be made of consultants' time.

80   In addition to the support that we envisage for all primary and special schools, we expect that the schools identified in the 10 to 15 per cent needing intensive support would also receive, in the school year 1999/2000:

- up to six days of visits to the school from the numeracy consultant;

- a five day training course for the mathematics co-ordinator and one other teacher, covering:

  - planning a series of day to day lessons in detail;
  - extending teaching skills, including questioning strategies;
  - additional training on teaching mental calculation methods;
  - additional training on teaching written calculation methods;
  - properties of numbers, number sequences, generalisations;
  - teaching fractions, decimals, percentages, ratio and proportion in Key Stage 2;
  - early years: Reception and Key Stage 1, including the use of number games and apparatus to give facility with number;
  - graphs and charts: from discrete to continuous data;
  - using the calculator with older pupils;
  - homework activities; and
  - planning and teaching demonstration lessons.

- some funding for classroom resources, which the LEA would delegate to schools following an audit of requirements, as described in the next chapter.

---

81   Some of the schools receiving the intensive support outlined above will continue to need it for a second year, perhaps even a third year. This extended intensive support should be available to up to 10% of schools. But the consultant will obviously be able to offer "intensive" support to further schools in 2000/2001 and 2001/2002. Over the three years of the strategy to 2002, close to 60% of all schools should be able to receive this level of support from the consultant.

82 We believe that our proposals for using the funding likely to be available for the strategy should, overall, allow for the whole of this 60% of schools to receive some direct support from a numeracy consultant in the first year of the strategy. Only 15% of these could receive the intensive support set out above in the first year, and up to 30% in any later year. The 45 % of these not receiving intensive support in the first year should, in that year, receive around 2 days of direct support from a consultant, to augment the basic training that we recommend for all schools. The support for these schools should focus on key parts of the training programme for schools receiving intensive support, including the teaching of written calculation methods, teaching fractions, decimals, percentages, ratio and proportion in Key Stage 2; and planning a series of day to day lessons in detail. It would also be open to these schools to use their own money for training to fund attendance by one or more teachers at the local 5 day course for schools receiving intensive support in that year, provided places are available.

Other schools

83 Schools that never fall into the category of "intensive" support could nonetheless receive a limited amount of "light touch" support from the consultant. As their varying needs demand, however, they should rely mainly on the national training materials, supplemented where appropriate by demonstration lessons taught by the local "leading mathematics teachers". As in the literacy strategy, the level of direct input that could be offered by a consultant to these schools would depend on the means by which this is offered. If a consultant offers a briefing session, perhaps with a demonstration lesson - whether as a twilight session, or as one of the INSET days, shared with other schools - several schools can be covered in one day. Visits to a school and direct support within normal lesson time naturally use more of the consultant's time. The detailed deployment of the consultant, and the way in which his or her input is supplemented by the local "leading mathematics teachers" should, in every case, be a decision for the LEA as part of its management of the strategy, in consultation with schools and the relevant Regional Director of the strategy.

DfEE support structure

84 LEAs responding to consultation thought it important to have good links between their schools as they implement the numeracy strategy, and between the LEAs and the DfEE. The professional development provided by the National Literacy Strategy is run by the DfEE through a National Director who is supported by Regional Directors plus a Director of Training. The Task Force believes that a similar structure should be provided for numeracy. These national and regional directors should be appointed as soon as possible, as it is important that support is in place from the beginning of 1999 to train the people who will, from the beginning of the summer term, act as consultants and "leading mathematics teachers".

85 Within the DfEE, the Literacy and Numeracy Strategy Group, which contains representation from key organisations and practising educators, will continue to oversee the implementation of both the literacy and numeracy strategies. As the National Numeracy Strategy begins in 1999, a key role of the Group will be to ensure coherence between the two strategies, and the different ways in which they will be supported by agencies such as OFSTED, QCA and TTA.

86 Our preliminary report asked whether the existing arrangements for consultation on issues affecting mathematics were adequate, and whether there was a need for any further mechanism to allow specific interest groups, such as parents or subject experts, to put their views. The major mathematical associations stressed that the special interrelated nature of mathematics creates a need for coherence in all aspects of mathematics education in this country. They expressed their eagerness to help in achieving this. They see a need for a small standing committee for mathematics education made up of subject experts. It would be worth giving further consideration to such a group, and to how it would relate to QCA, OFSTED, TTA and the Literacy and Numeracy Strategy Group. We recognise that the setting up of such a group could have implications for other curriculum subjects.

LEA management of the strategy

87 As with the National Literacy Strategy, the Task Force expects that whilst the numeracy consultants will be answerable to the National Director and relevant Regional Director, and be in close contact with the latter, they will be line managed within the LEA. It is important that schools perceive any LEA initiatives to improve numeracy standards, and other support, such as SEN or EAL support, or support for gifted and talented pupils, as forming a seamless whole with the National Numeracy Strategy. We would expect that, given the importance of this strategy, a key part of all LEA advisers' jobs will be supporting and complementing it through training and other activities. In particular, as noted in the section above about numeracy consultants, the LEA will need to provide additional support to consultants when dealing with those schools who need most help in implementing the strategy. They will also have a role in providing certain specialist expertise, for example, helping consultants in running training. LEAs should ensure immediately that they have in post someone with the right management experience and mathematical skills to perform this role, and should organise conferences to enable their staff to become familiar with the strategy.

88 As with the National Literacy Strategy, as part of their bid for Standards Fund funding, a key role of the LEA should be to negotiate targets with the DfEE that will ultimately feed into the national target of 75% of children reaching Level 4 in 2002. The Task Force is encouraged by the fact that no LEA has set a 2002 literacy target that is lower than the target range suggested to them by the DfEE. We hope that LEAs' numeracy targets would be similarly ambitious, yet realistic.

89 Under regulations to come into effect in September 1998, governing bodies will be required to set targets for the performance of the 11 year olds in their schools every year. These statutory targets will apply to performance in mathematics and English only. Schools will of course be setting targets in other areas as they see fit, but there is no statutory duty on them to do so. Under other regulations, LEAs will also be required to have a three-year Education Development Plan (EDP) in place by April 1999. An EDP will have to contain certain LEA pupil performance targets and the school improvement programme to achieve those targets, both of which will be subject to the approval of the Secretary of State. The mandatory targets will include performance in mathematics and English. The targets for 2002 should be consistent with the targets that we propose and should be agreed between DfEE and every LEA as part of the National Numeracy Strategy. LEAs will need to give evidence of satisfactory rates of improvement and attainment each year, and may, if they wish, provide additional supporting information, which could include further targets related to numeracy. This supporting information will not, however, be subject to approval by the Secretary of State.

90 It should be the responsibility of schools to set their own mathematics targets showing how the school will play its part in reaching the LEA's target for 2002. LEAs should encourage schools to set challenging but realistic targets through a process of discussion about the school's strengths and weaknesses, the abilities of their 2002 cohort and where they hope to be in 2002. It is important that the target setting process is one of genuine negotiation between the school and LEA. The DfEE is currently consulting on the first draft of the statutory *Code of Practice on LEA-School Relations*, which will contain further guidance on target setting with schools. Schools and LEAs should begin the process of agreeing targets as early as possible. If this is done well, it should help to prepare schools for the more detailed audit and target setting exercise that we recommend for summer 1999.

Special schools

91 The assumption in the Task Force's preliminary report, that the strategy should involve special schools as far as possible, has been widely welcomed. We recognise and welcome the fact that, increasingly, children with special educational needs are in mainstream classrooms, and would expect these children to participate in the daily mathematics lesson with the rest of the class. This issue is explored in more depth in the next chapter, which deals with the strategy in schools, including the practicalities of teaching the daily mathematics lesson. We recognise that special schools are a heterogeneous sector, currently in a state of change and development. We believe that special schools with pupils in Key Stages 1 and 2 should also play a full part in the National Numeracy Strategy, and receive the training and support we envisage for all schools. It is becoming evident from work in the NNP in Coventry and Birmingham that the principles on which our strategy is based can be adapted to the special school environment, and examples of this should be made available in the training materials.

92 One key adaptation is the notion of "whole class teaching", in which the classroom organisation is different from that in a mainstream primary school. In a special school, there may be 12 to 14 pupils in a class, with the class teacher supported at times by other staff. There may be times when all of these pupils are taught together for their daily mathematics lesson, just as in a mainstream primary school. At other times, two "whole class" lessons may be taking place in the same room, with the class teacher working with one half of the class and the support teacher with the other half. In all cases, however, the emphases in the strategy on oral work and mental calculation, some daily mental practice, and keeping children working together as far as reasonable, still apply. Key resources, such as number lines, will also be used to the full. Other adaptations to the daily mathematics lesson will include, for example, the pace at which the teacher conducts oral work when working with children who are deaf, or have hearing impairments, the use of signing, symbols or special aids to support communication, or the duration of independent group work for pupils with emotional and behavioural difficulties.

93 There is also scope for adapting the *Framework for teaching* to suit special schools in a way that will advance and consolidate children's learning of mathematics without sacrificing the breadth of the Framework, or the principle of planning from clearly defined objectives. For example, it may be appropriate for a special school to base its work for primary aged children on the yearly teaching programmes in the Framework covering Reception and Years 1 and 2, for example, taking two years to cover one of the yearly programmes. Some aspects of the Framework, such as termly discussions with individual children to set them personal targets, will need no adaptation, since they are already well established in special schools. The Framework should also help both mainstream and special school teachers prepare individual education plans (IEPs) for those pupils who need them.

94 As noted above, the National Numeracy Strategy should begin with three days of training for all headteachers, co-ordinators, a governor, and another teacher from each primary and special school. As with the National Literacy Strategy, we believe that this initial training would be valuable for all special schools. If numbers make it feasible, however, we recommend that LEAs arrange for staff from some special schools to be trained together, or at least have one or more sessions within a more general conference together. We have suggested above that day 2 of the initial conference would be most suitable for this purpose, where special schools have specific needs that could not easily be addressed in sessions with mainstream schools. This would allow them to ask questions, and be given answers, that are specifically tailored to their individual circumstances.

95 Most of the material to be used in the INSET days for all schools will be as applicable to special schools as it is to primary schools - guidance on any necessary adaptations should be included in the pack. Where an LEA judges that a special school would benefit from more intensive training in the teaching of mathematics, it would be valuable for special school teachers to attend the 5 day training course for mainstream schools receiving intensive support. It might, however, be helpful to develop some supplementary training modules, on the use of, for example, specialised teaching and learning aids in mathematics. We also envisage that consultants will give direct support to special schools, but that this will vary according to the particular needs of their pupils, and the way they will need to adapt the Framework and the daily mathematics lesson. In all cases, this support will need to be planned in partnership between the LEA's special needs advisers.

Continuing professional development

96 At the heart of our proposed National Numeracy Strategy is a programme of training for all primary schools and special schools in the most effective methods of teaching mathematics. This will entitle all teachers to an opportunity to acquire basic knowledge and skills that will enable them to teach mathematics effectively in the primary classroom. But a national strategy to improve standards of mathematics cannot stop here. As we have already noted, the 2002 target of 75% of 11 year olds reaching Level 4 is a staging post on the way to the aim of virtually all 11 year olds reaching this standard by around 2007, and all pupils making appropriate progress. It was clear from consultation responses that whilst a strategy to raise standards to 2002 is both welcome and important, this needs to be backed up by a continuing commitment on the part of government, LEAs, schools and individual teachers, to continual improvement and extension of teaching skills. Continuing professional development is not, of course, solely a matter of attending INSET courses. Teachers can learn a lot by working alongside their colleagues, sharing good practice and finding common solutions to common problems. The emphasis in our recommended strategy on the importance of teachers demonstrating good practice for their colleagues shows how important we believe this type of continuing professional development to be.

97 The Task Force is concerned about teachers' worries, in their responses to consultation, about weaknesses in their basic subject knowledge in mathematics. It is not necessary for an effective primary teacher of mathematics to have advanced qualifications in mathematics, but as we stated in our preliminary report, it is important that primary teachers know about the primary mathematics curriculum, including how different topics relate to and support one another, as required in the ITT National Curriculum for primary mathematics, and how this knowledge will support children's later development of mathematical skills. Teachers also need to know how best to teach mathematics so that their pupils learn and apply it. We are convinced that the basics of our strategy will have a considerable effect on many teachers' subject knowledge. It is clear from the NNP that simply familiarising teachers with the teaching objectives in the *Framework for teaching*, and giving them the help and opportunity to use the Framework in their daily teaching of mathematics, allows teachers to develop greater confidence in their subject knowledge. In short, teachers may not realise the subject knowledge that they already have, and underestimate the extent to which lively interaction with their class about mathematics, with good quality material to support their teaching, will increase their own knowledge as well as that of their pupils. But as teachers gain further confidence and become more effective, they are, if anything, better equipped to see how this basic package of knowledge and skills needs to be enhanced to further their subject knowledge in specific areas.

98 With the introduction of the National Curriculum for initial teacher training in primary mathematics in September this year, newly-qualified teachers should begin to enter the profession from September 1999 with a more secure subject knowledge. They will also have received training in the classroom use of new technologies. We believe that the National Numeracy Strategy will help to establish a climate in which all teachers have a desire to acquire new knowledge and improve their teaching and subject knowledge constantly. Our long-term aspiration is for all teachers of primary aged-children, and secondary teachers of mathematics, to receive the equivalent of 5 days of training in the subject-specific and generic skills of teaching mathematics, over the five years from 2000. Those with responsibility for leading mathematics within schools should seek out training that equips them for this particular role, and deepens their knowledge of what makes for effective mathematics teaching, perhaps by carrying out research. This continuing professional development is important for all teachers, but we recognise that those primary teachers, especially co-ordinators, who do not have qualifications in mathematics beyond GCSE, are likely to be less confident about their subject knowledge in mathematics. This also applies to secondary mathematics teachers without a post A-level mathematics qualification. We recognise that we will have set an ambitious target, and that the DfEE will need to consider its substantial resource implications. Some of this funding could form part of the continued support for the National Numeracy Strategy, after the review in 2002 of progress towards our proposed target. This longer term strategy, to ensure that all classroom teachers have the knowledge and skills to teach mathematics effectively, should:

- build on lessons learned in previous INSET, including the five to twenty day mathematics courses funded through the DfEE's Grants for Education Support and Training (GEST) programme;

- relate to teachers' assessments of their individual needs, drawing wherever appropriate on the TTA's needs assessment materials;

- set out clearly the standards to be attained, building on the TTA's professional standards;

- make use of the expertise built up in HE, and in LEAs by mathematics advisory staff and, wherever possible, in a continuing role for the numeracy consultants recruited to support the National Numeracy Strategy;

- make effective use of new guidance and teaching materials available through the National Grid for Learning and of the Beacon Schools programme; and

- include monitoring and evaluation of the effects of the training on teaching and learning in the classroom.

99 The aim of these criteria is to ensure continuing professional development of high quality, specifically planned to address teachers' areas of concern, in order to have real impact on standards in the classroom. The TTA's professional framework for teachers aims to help teachers at different points in their careers to plan and monitor their development, training and performance effectively and to set clear targets for improvement. It seeks to focus at every point on improving pupils' achievement and the general quality of education. The sets of national standards set out the professional knowledge, understanding, skills and attributes necessary for teachers to carry out key aspects of their role effectively. They emphasise the government's national priorities of literacy, numeracy and information and communication technology (ICT). Since the Task Force's preliminary report, the TTA has published its needs assessment materials for Key Stage 2 mathematics. These materials should be useful in helping with the process of planning for professional development by identifying areas of subject knowledge with which teachers need help. Other standards published by the TTA, including those for training of headteachers, subject leaders and SENCOs, should also take account of the role of these individuals in supporting numeracy.

100 HMCI's 1996-1997 annual report states that, in one in six primary schools, INSET was poorly matched to the needs of staff. It also indicates that appraisal is well-established in fewer than half of the schools, and has yet to make a serious impact on the quality of teaching in the majority of schools. Whilst this shows that many schools are making good use of their INSET, and that there is a good start on appraisal in some schools, there is clearly room for improvement if children are to attain high standards of achievement. We hope that this strategy will be the catalyst for improvement in mathematics.

101 The Task Force is aware that further development work is taking place on appraisal before new arrangements are put in place for September 1999. We welcome the emphasis that is being placed on focused professional development and objectives related to pupils' performance. We hope that the guidance materials, on which development work has begun, and the regulations governing the arrangements, on which consultation is planned for spring 1999, will make clear to LEAs and schools, in a practical way, how they can establish links between planning for whole school improvement and individual professional development.

Providers of Initial Teacher Training (ITT)

102 The Task Force expects that the daily mathematics lesson, based on the good practice that our strategy seeks to bring about, would become the norm in primary and special schools. It is therefore essential for the continuing success of the strategy in raising standards that new teachers enter the profession fully informed about the National Numeracy Strategy and equipped to teach the daily mathematics lesson. We recognised in our preliminary report that a key to long term improvements in numeracy is the recruitment and training of future teachers. Providers of ITT should teach trainees about the National Numeracy Strategy, as part of the new ITT National Curriculum for primary mathematics. The providers have a crucial role in ensuring that these new teachers enter the classroom with levels of knowledge, skills and understanding that will allow them to teach mathematics well to primary aged pupils.

103 We welcome the emphasis on numeracy skills in the National Curriculum for ITT in primary mathematics. It is obviously important that all ITT providers should be sent copies of the *Framework for teaching*, and a continuing supply should be made available so that new trainees can receive a copy. We believe that any staff in higher education who work closely with primary and special schools, as well as ITT providers, should all be well informed about the National Numeracy Strategy. Many will provide further professional development programmes for teachers and will have a role in promoting the strategy's principles and practices in schools, and in extending knowledge of ICT applications in the teaching of numeracy. Others will be engaged in research that relates directly to the effective teaching of numeracy. We therefore believe that conferences should be arranged, similar to those held earlier this summer for ITT providers to explore issues relating to the National Literacy Strategy. The DfEE and the TTA should organise these conferences in the summer term of 1999, in preparation for the implementation of the National Numeracy Strategy in the autumn.

104 These conferences should:

> - ensure that conference delegates are well-informed about the National Numeracy Strategy, including the *Framework for teaching*, and are clear about their own role in its implementation;
>
> - ensure that conference delegates are fully aware of the implications of the strategy for trainee teachers and those already in the classroom;
>
> - emphasise the importance of mathematics within ITT, induction and continuing professional development programmes;
>
> - pay attention to the continuing professional development needs of teachers implementing the National Numeracy Strategy; and
>
> - consider the further research that could best help to improve teaching of mathematics and raise standards of numeracy.

Recommendations

The DfEE should

summer 1998

- undertake further development of the *Framework for teaching*, in the light of the input given by senior members of mathematics associations, and further input from QCA, TTA, and OFSTED;

- begin recruiting national and regional support staff for the National Numeracy Strategy, with the intention of having all these appointed no later than the end of December 1998;

- inform LEAs of the number of numeracy consultant posts the DfEE can guarantee to fund from 1 April 1999, asking them to recruit by the end of December 1998 to have them in post by 1 April 1999;

- begin work on the production of a specification for training courses; and

- begin to consider whether and how a standing committee for mathematics education might complement existing mechanisms.

autumn term 1998

- prepare training programmes and materials for inducting consultants and preparing "leading mathematics teachers" for their role;

- begin development work on materials for three day training courses, and distance learning materials for whole school INSET, particularly video material to show successful teaching of the daily mathematics lesson;

- as part of the Standards Fund bidding process, agree targets for Key Stage 2 mathematics, and local action plans to improve standards of mathematics, with all LEAs, to include their plans for phasing of support for schools and particularly for those to receive intensive support; and

- provide induction for Regional Directors of the strategy.

spring term 1999

- send copies of the *Framework for teaching* to all teachers in primary, middle and special schools, LEAs, at least one copy to all secondary schools, and a reasonable number of copies to all ITT providers, ensuring that a continuing supply is printed;

- fund training for people identified to take up numeracy consultant posts and for the "leading mathematics teachers" who will support schools when the strategy begins, the training to be run in regions by the strategy's Regional Directors;

- organise conferences for LEA advisers and support staff to familiarise them with the training materials and discuss the support they will need to provide for consultants and schools; and

- prepare training materials and programmes for the 5 day training courses for schools receiving intensive support.

- with the TTA, hold regional conferences for INSET and ITT providers to familiarise them with the strategy, particularly the Framework; and

- consult on adding an "average level score" for primary pupils at the end of Key Stage 2 to future school performance tables, for mathematics.

autumn term 1999

- with the TTA, draw up plans to facilitate the continuing professional development of teachers of mathematics.

LEAs should:

autumn term 1998

- build up and organise existing clusters and other local networks of schools, and encourage new ones, with a view to creating opportunities for sharing good practice;

- identify mathematics co-ordinators and teachers who have a particular strength in teaching mathematics who can act as "leading mathematics teachers", to support schools when the strategy begins;

- ensure that they have in post someone with the management experience and mathematical skills to line manage consultants and provide extra support for training;

- advertise for, and recruit, numeracy consultants in line with DfEE guidelines, by the end of December 1998, to take up post from 1 April 1999;

- liaise with the DfEE and consultants' existing employers to secure sufficient release for them in the spring term to undertake induction training; and

- agree a Key Stage 2 mathematics target for 2002, and an action plan for raising standards of numeracy, with the DfEE.

spring term 1999

- assist the DfEE's Regional Directors in running and supplementing training for the numeracy consultants who will start work in April, and for the "leading mathematics teachers";

- negotiate and agree Key Stage 2 mathematics targets with schools, that will feed into the LEA target;

- send SEN line managers and support staff to the DfEE conferences on the numeracy strategy; and

- identify the schools that will need the most intensive support in the first year of the strategy.

summer term 1999

- facilitate arrangements for teachers to watch demonstration lessons taught by a consultant or a "leading mathematics teacher"; and

- run three day conferences for headteachers, mathematics co-ordinators, one other teacher, and a governor from all primary and special schools.

Primary and middle schools and, where appropriate, special schools, should:

autumn term 1998

- if they have not already done so, identify a teacher who will act as mathematics co-ordinator, who should take advantage of any suitable training or briefing opportunities that come up in the time leading up to the strategy implementation, and take responsibility, with the headteacher, for familiarising themselves with the National Numeracy Strategy.

spring term 1999

- agree a Key Stage 2 mathematics target for 2002 with their LEA.

summer term 1999

- send the headteacher, mathematics co-ordinator and one other experienced teacher, who could usefully be the SENCO, on the initial 3 day training course, with a governor attending for at least the third day;

- audit their current practice in mathematics, including classroom resources, to support the introduction of the daily mathematics lesson, and spend any Standards Fund grant delegated from the LEA accordingly; and

- devote one INSET day, after the initial training course, to a whole school training event to prepare for teaching the daily mathematics lesson the following term.

autumn term 1999

- early in the term, facilitate observation of demonstration lessons, either "live" or on video;

- devote an INSET day early in the term to further training on the daily mathematics lesson;

- establish the daily mathematics lesson in all classrooms, and begin to allow time for the mathematics co-ordinator and, where appropriate, other colleagues, to work with teachers to implement the changes in practice; and

- schools receiving intensive support to send the mathematics co-ordinator and another teacher on a further course.

spring and summer terms 2000

- devote another INSET day to further training to improve the daily mathematics lesson; and

- continue to ensure that the mathematics co-ordinator and, where appropriate, other colleagues, have time to work with colleagues in the classroom (e.g. by teaching demonstration lessons) to sustain the successful implementation of the daily lesson.

OFSTED should:

autumn term 1998

- provide guidance for inspectors on inspecting numeracy, to be subsequently made available to schools.

summer term 1999

- run training for inspectors about the National Numeracy Strategy.

autumn term 1999

- undertake visits to a significant sample of schools to begin the evaluation of the strategy.

TTA should:

summer 1998

- ensure that national standards for headteachers, subject leaders and SENCOs take account of their respective roles in developing numeracy skills.

The strategy in schools

Mathematics in the National Curriculum

105 The Task Force's preliminary report acknowledged that the detailed content of the mathematics curriculum was for QCA to recommend to Ministers in the light of its review of the National Curriculum, which will be completed in 1999, with the revised curriculum coming into force from September 2000. It is important that QCA takes into account in this review the experience of schools in working with the current curriculum, the work of the NNP and other projects to raise standards of primary mathematics, and successful practice in other countries, which the Task Force has distilled into its recommendations for a national strategy. We gave a strong message for the QCA review in our preliminary report. We said that the curriculum should have a greater emphasis on oral work and mental calculation, because it was clear from the evidence we studied that this was the best means of ensuring that children had a good grounding in numeracy. We thought it was important that the curriculum made explicit when formal written calculation methods were to be introduced, and that this should be when these foundations were secure. These recommendations have received a strong welcome in consultation responses, and we therefore reiterate and emphasise them in this final report.

106 The final version of the *Framework for teaching* should be made available to all primary teachers. The Framework is designed to help teachers teach the National Curriculum for mathematics. It sets out teaching objectives year by year, showing how to plan and pace work, so that emphasis is given to numeracy in the overall mathematics programme. In particular, the Framework sets out to establish oral and mental competence before written calculation methods are introduced. It is therefore essential that the review of the National Curriculum for primary mathematics should proceed, as far as possible, in parallel with finalisation of the *Framework for teaching*.

Mental and written calculations

107 Responses to consultation confirmed the Task Force's view in *Numeracy Matters* that mental calculation methods lie at the heart of numeracy. They should be emphasised from an early age, but the balance between mental and written methods, and the way in which pupils progress from one to the other, are both very important. The *Framework for teaching* identifies a clear progression that avoids the premature teaching of standard written methods, and which teachers can use to plan an appropriate approach.

108 From Reception onwards, children should be encouraged to move from practical work to the abstract – thinking with numbers alone. At first, they can be shown the idea of adding or subtracting a number using real objects, then asked to visualise the objects, use different representations of them, and say what they think the answer is. Children will work out their answers in different ways, depending on the numbers involved. After sufficient experience with a variety of situations, real and imaginary, and problems posed in different ways, children should be taught to remember and recall, say, that five add three is eight, or that seven taken from nine leaves two. These early stages of mental calculation are not, however, at the exclusion of written recording. When children can read and write numerals, they should start to use correct notation to complete calculations such as $5 + 8 = \square$ or $13 = \square + 5$. In this way, they can begin to appreciate the economy of mathematical symbols.

109 As pupils progress to working with larger numbers, they will learn more sophisticated mental methods and tackle more complex problems. They will develop some of these methods intuitively and will be taught some of them explicitly. Through a process of regular explanation and discussion of their own and other children's methods, they will begin to acquire a repertoire of mental calculation strategies. At this stage, it can be hard for them to hold all the intermediate steps in their heads, and so informal pencil and paper notes, recording some or all of their solutions, become part of a mental strategy.

These personal jottings may not be easy for someone else to follow, but they are a staging post to getting the right answer and to acquiring fluency in mental calculation. By discussing and comparing different part written, part mental methods, pupils are guided towards choosing those that are most efficient and which can be applied generally. At this point, the need for more formal recording of calculation methods emerges.

110 Standard written methods offer reliable and efficient procedures which, once mastered, can be used in many different contexts. They are no use, however, to someone who applies them inaccurately, and who cannot judge whether the answer is reasonable. For each operation at least one standard written method of calculation should be taught in primary schools, but the progression towards these methods is crucial. This is because they are based on steps that are done mentally and need to be secured first.

111 When it has reviewed the mathematics curriculum, QCA should provide guidance for schools on teaching written methods of calculation. The guidance should give advice on what kind of written strategies should be taught and the stage at which these are most appropriately introduced.

The use of calculators

112 The use of calculators is not an issue on its own, but the principles governing when and how calculators should be used flow from our view of the importance of oral and mental work as the central focus for pupils acquiring numeracy skills. All respondents recognised that the Task Force's emphasis on this work had implications for the use of calculators in primary classrooms, and generally agreed that the use of calculators should be limited, particularly for younger pupils. They confirmed our belief that greater emphasis should be given in primary classrooms to oral and mental work in the teaching of numeracy.

113 Respondents were keen to have further advice on how and when calculators should be used in the classroom. The Task Force believes that calculators are best used in primary schools in the later years of Key Stage 2. When calculators are introduced, they need to be used properly, or their value is lost. There is no place in primary school mathematics lessons for using calculators as a prop for simple arithmetic, since children are still learning the mental calculation skills and written methods that they will need throughout their lives. Used well, however, calculators can be an effective tool for learning about numbers and the number system, such as place value, precision, and fractions and decimals, perhaps with the teacher using an overhead projector calculator to demonstrate to the whole class. Calculators can also play an important part in subjects such as science, geography or history, by allowing children to use real data gathered in experiments or research, which will often contain numbers that make calculations more difficult.

114 Once children reach secondary school, teachers should be able to take it for granted that they are able to use a calculator properly to handle arithmetical operations, which makes it very important for primary schools not only to use the calculator appropriately, but to teach children the technical skills needed to use it constructively and efficiently, such as being able to use a calculator's memory to store information when undertaking calculations that involve several steps. Children also need to be taught when it is, and is not, appropriate to use a calculator. This is an important element of the definition of numeracy, quoted at the beginning of our preliminary report and this report. Children's first strategy in the classroom should be to use mental calculation skills whenever possible. They should understand a calculation well enough to decide whether it is best to use their mental skills, write it down or use a calculator to work out the answer. Children should also have a sense of the approximate size of the answer they expect to get when using a calculator, and know how to check the answer if they are not sure whether it is right.

115 The Task Force is aware that the speed of change in technology, and its increasing accessibility for schools, are issues that cannot be ignored in mathematics teaching. The distinction between a computer and a calculator is rapidly becoming blurred. Relatively cheap calculators can now display graphics, and can be programmed and linked to a computer to transfer data and software. Teachers now have access to hand-held computers, which do all that a calculator is expected to do, but which can also run software previously available on desk-top computers. We believe that these developments make it all the more important that young children acquire the numeracy skills they need to access the technology they will use in later life, and that they leave primary school able to make judicious and effective use of the basic functions of the calculator.

116 A key message to emerge from consultation was that many teachers are anxious to receive advice on the appropriate way to use calculators. QCA is currently preparing guidance for teachers on mental calculation strategies. This will also indicate when and how calculators can be most effectively used, ensuring that pupils' mental calculation strategies are properly developed first. The Task Force has contributed to the preparation of this guidance. It is important that QCA continues to ensure, as the *Framework for teaching* is finalised, that this guidance reflects the Framework and the revised mathematics curriculum, and can be presented to schools as complementary support material within the National Numeracy Strategy. It should be sent to schools at the same time as the Framework.

The daily mathematics lesson

117 Since the publication of the Task Force's preliminary report in January, Ministers have given schools greater flexibility in the compulsory curriculum for Key Stages 1 and 2, so that they will have more time to concentrate on English and mathematics from September 1998, when the daily literacy hour is introduced. This greater flexibility will allow them to spend an hour each day on literacy and up to an hour on mathematics, as we recommend, and most schools will no doubt begin to teach a daily lesson from September 1998. From September 1999, when the numeracy strategy starts, primary and special schools should teach this daily mathematics lesson using the structure and methods set out at the beginning of this report. It is important that teachers teaching the daily lesson, particularly where this constitutes a major change in practice, should be properly trained and supported. We believe that the recommendations in the previous chapter should ensure that this happens. It will take time for every teacher to be wholly confident and effective in teaching the daily lesson. We hope that the structure would certainly be used fully as a basis for teaching mathematics in every primary classroom, and many special school classrooms, by the autumn half term. Schools should then continue to improve their delivery of the lesson throughout the school year 1999/2000, and beyond.

118   As noted in our preliminary report, providing a daily mathematics lesson for all primary and special school pupils will be a major step in ensuring equal access to regular, sustained teaching of mathematics. This will allow children regular practice of mental calculation strategies and recall of key number facts, such as multiplication tables. Lessons should be supplemented by weekly homework activities for all children, set in accordance with the DfEE's guidelines on good practice in homework, on which schools have been consulted. The daily lesson should normally be based on the structure we recommend in chapter 1, which has been used successfully in the NNP. As the diagram in chapter 1 shows, this includes a high proportion of whole class teaching, as well as some work in groups, in pairs and individually, the blend of methods recommended in our preliminary report. It is most important to ensure that the detailed structure of any particular lesson fits the overall purpose of the lesson, and that a suitable pace is maintained throughout. It is particularly important for the whole class to be together at the beginning and end of the lesson, so that the objectives for the lesson can be made clear, and, at the end, the teacher and pupils can sum up together what has been learnt, and correct any errors or misconceptions.

Differentiation

Dealing with a range of attainment

119   It is clear from inspection and other evidence that the range of attainment in mathematics in many classrooms, particularly at the upper end of Key Stage 2, is currently too wide. The aim of our recommended strategy is to allow all the children in a class to progress steadily, so that all of them reach a satisfactory standard and the range of attainment is much narrower. We are concerned that children should not continue to work at many different levels, with the teacher placing them in a wide range of differentiated groups. We have recommended a daily mathematics lesson for all primary schools, and where appropriate, special schools, in which the whole class is taught

together for a high proportion of the time. The teacher should be able to spend more time interacting directly with the class about mathematics, and less time than many teachers do at present in troubleshooting with individuals. It is important to remember, however, that although the structure of the daily mathematics lesson envisages that all the children in a class will work on the same topic at the same time, there is a certain amount of differentiation in the group work in the structure outlined in chapter 1, and in targeted questions for individual children during whole class work.

120   This differentiation within the whole class, for part of the lesson, is an effective means of dealing with the range of attainment that will inevitably exist in any classroom. We are aware that some schools also deal with this by organising mathematics teaching in ability sets. When considering the scope for setting pupils, it is important for schools to remember that setting does not necessarily help to close the overall range in attainment across sets over time. Some pupils may become discouraged when they are placed in a lower set, so schools that decide to place children in sets need to monitor the arrangements carefully and continuously. Schools should ensure that parents understand the reasons why a school has decided to set pupils for mathematics, especially if this is not happening in other subjects. In particular, good teamwork and co-operative planning is needed to ensure the transfer of children between sets. Perhaps the most important consideration is our aspiration for the gap in attainment between pupils to become smaller over time, and particularly for under-achieving pupils to improve their standards of achievement, as our strategy makes an impact. We know that teachers share this aspiration, and they should remember that it means that over time, setting may need to be used less as the range of attainment narrows.

121   The Task Force does, nonetheless, recognise the concerns that teachers have about applying a structure with a good deal of whole class teaching if they have a high number of pupils with SEN or EAL in a class, or if there is an unusually large range of attainment in one class. Responses to consultation also showed concern about ensuring that very able pupils are stretched in whole class teaching, and about applying this model in very small schools with mixed age classes. We believe that the experience of the NNP provides a good foundation for addressing these concerns, and have expanded our comments on these issues to reflect that experience. The national materials produced for the strategy should include further guidance on these matters, building wherever possible on any similar guidance that is produced during the first year of the National Literacy Strategy.

Pupils with special educational needs in mainstream classrooms

122   The national drive for early, high quality intervention in both literacy and numeracy is intended to reduce the number of children who need long term provision for SEN. We have been particularly encouraged by the progress of pupils with SEN, including some with statements, in schools taking part in the NNP. Teachers have generally aimed to

keep children with SEN up with the general pace of teaching in the class, rather than to offer a high degree of differentiated work. They have done this with children with a range of SEN, including moderate learning or behavioural difficulties, or physical disabilities or impairments, and as a result, many of the children whose development had been delayed have begun to catch up. The basic training programme we have recommended for all schools as part of the National Numeracy Strategy should highlight the teaching strategies and resources that teachers can use to help children like this, including ways of identifying and correcting children's misconceptions.

123 There may, however, be a small proportion of children in mainstream schools who suffer from severe difficulties that seriously hamper their progress in mathematics. The most common of these difficulties is problems with memorising and recalling facts. Other difficulties can include an inability to understand and apply methods of calculating, and visual/spatial difficulty in representing and interpreting arithmetical information. Children who have these extreme difficulties are likely to be referred for an assessment of their special educational needs. As stated in our preliminary report, we believe it is very important that numeracy, as well as literacy, is addressed in these children's statements and individual education plans (IEPs), so that teachers can plan activities that suit the children's needs. All these children should participate in at least part of the daily mathematics lesson with other members of their class. In the middle part of the lesson, children with severe difficulties with mathematics should follow an individualised programme with appropriate support, but would benefit from being included in the oral work with the whole class at the beginning and end of the daily lesson.

124 The Task Force acknowledges that the inclusion of pupils with SEN in the daily mathematics lesson in mainstream primary schools will pose particular challenges for teachers. At the same time, however, we believe our recommended strategy offers real opportunities for allowing these children to improve their numeracy skills and work with and learn from other children. With this in mind, it would be helpful for the SENCO to attend the initial three day training course we have recommended as the start of the National Numeracy Strategy, with the headteacher, mathematics co-ordinator, and governor, especially if the primary school has a very high proportion of pupils on the SEN register, or is specially resourced for SEN. The SENCO should also be given opportunities to work with the mathematics co-ordinator and other colleagues to support the teaching of mathematics for pupils with SEN.

Pupils who are very able

125 There was some concern expressed in consultation that the emphasis on whole class teaching would not sufficiently stretch pupils who are very able. We recognise this concern, and acknowledge the importance of ensuring that levelling up as many children as possible does not result in the most able children being held back. There are two ways of catering for these children - either by enriching the curriculum for them

through harder problems or puzzles, or by accelerating them through it. The training and other support provided to schools as part of the National Numeracy Strategy should help teachers to cater for these children effectively in the context of the daily mathematics lesson.

126 The great majority of very able pupils in mathematics are taught with their own class in the NNP. During whole class sessions in the daily mathematics lesson, the teacher directs some questions towards the pupils in the class who are most able, in the same way that some questions are directed towards those who find mathematics most difficult. These pupils can be stretched through differentiated work in the sessions of group work, extra challenges they can do towards the end of a topic when other pupils are working through exercises to consolidate their understanding, and harder problems given to them for homework. The teaching programmes in the *Framework for teaching* leave a period amounting to about one week in each term that is unallocated. This time could be used for the most able to carry out a sustained mathematical investigation, such as those that can be downloaded from the Internet from the NRICH website, which we mentioned in our preliminary report.

127 Pupils who are exceptionally gifted in many subjects, and who are sufficiently mature, are commonly promoted to work with an older age group. Typically, these pupils are able to deal with abstract mathematics much earlier than other children, and for them, some acceleration is desirable. Very occasionally, a pupil may be exceptionally gifted at mathematics, but not in other subjects. These pupils should still participate in the daily mathematics lesson, but schools can make special arrangements to accommodate them, for example, by timetabling Years 3 and 4 mathematics lessons at the same time, so that a gifted Year 3 pupil can easily be taught mathematics within the Year 4 class, and benefit, during co-operative group work, from discussion with other pupils at a similar level of attainment. Where this is not possible, exceptionally gifted pupils can follow individualised programmes at appropriate times within the daily lesson, in the same way as a pupil with very severe difficulties with mathematics, and in this way work more quickly through the mainstream course.

Small schools

128 Quite a large number of respondents to consultation mentioned the particular difficulty of implementing a daily mathematics lesson with a high proportion of whole class teaching in a very small school. Such a school typically has only two or three teachers, and therefore cannot avoid teaching all together pupils of a wide range of ages, and therefore attainments. We are encouraged by the fact that the NNP has been successful in a range of settings, from small rural schools to large inner city primary schools. The Task Force believes it should be possible to replicate this success nationally across a similar range of schools, and that examples of using our recommended lesson structure in small schools should be included in the video training material discussed in the previous chapter. We would recommend, however, that where schools have parallel mixed-age classes from choice rather than from necessity, they should reorganise them into year groups for mathematics, as planning and teaching are easier if the attainment gap in any one class is not too wide.

129 In the NNP, classes containing children from two different year groups are taught mathematics in the same way as classes with a single year group. When teachers are questioning the class, for example, they make sure that they include questions targeted at particular pupils or groups of pupils. During group work, teachers tend to aim for four groups - an upper and middle group of older children and a middle and lower group of younger children - but plan work at three levels, so that the two middle groups do the same work. When different groups give feedback during the plenary session, the children have a common interest as they have all been working on the same topic, albeit at different levels of difficulty.

130 Very small schools may be obliged to include three or more year groups in one class. Schools in this situation should still ensure that the main theme of the lesson is based on the same topic for all children, but the teacher may need to plan tasks for group work at four, or even five levels of difficulty, rather than three, with the children allocated to a group based on the activity that is most suitable for them. In the NNP, classes of this kind are often organised in two halves for direct teaching, with the children whom the teacher will be teaching directly on a particular day sitting closest to the chalk board. Whilst this half of the class is being taught directly, the other half works independently of the teacher on the tasks planned for them.

131 The main purpose of the initial part of the daily mathematics lesson, which involves oral work and mental calculation, is to rehearse recall skills and keep them sharp. In very small schools, this instruction can be included in the direct teaching time in the mathematics lesson for each half of the class, or one or both halves of the class can have this part of the lesson at any convenient time of the day.

Mathematics across the primary curriculum

132 The references in our preliminary report to the scope for promoting pupils' numeracy skills across other subjects was welcomed in consultation. Whilst primary schools have now been given greater flexibility to decide what to teach in history, geography, design and technology, music, art and PE, pending the outcome of the National Curriculum review in 2000, they retain a statutory duty to provide their pupils with a broad and balanced curriculum. The Task Force fully supports this principle, whilst recognising that without competence in the vital basic skills of literacy and numeracy, children will simply be unable to benefit from the opportunities that a broad and balanced curriculum offers. A national strategy to improve pupils' numeracy is therefore important if this curriculum is to be a reality.

133 At the same time, we believe, as stated in *Numeracy Matters*, that other subjects offer a rich source of opportunities for children to consolidate and practise what they have learnt in mathematics lessons, and to extend those skills further. In the literacy hour, children can read books that include mathematical data. In history, for example, children can use time lines or gather data and then present the data in a graph chart or table. In geography, children can use co-ordinates, compass directions and bearings, and gather data by measuring, then present it. In art, children can look at the properties of shapes and patterns, including symmetry, and in PE, children can measure distance, time and speed. The numeracy strategy should help primary schools define and exploit these opportunities even more effectively than they do at present.

Assessment

134 The Task Force identified in its preliminary report how high quality formative assessment by teachers can make an important contribution to helping pupils improve their numeracy skills. The effective use of assessment has been shown to make a significant impact in raising the standards of attainment overall. In *Numeracy Matters*, we identified in particular the importance of:

- gathering information about each pupil's strengths and weaknesses, whether from formal or informal tests, responses in class discussions, performance in problem - solving or investigation tasks in which pupils apply their knowledge;

- agreeing personal targets with each pupil, and discussing and reviewing their progress towards them;

- giving constructive feedback, which will enable pupils to improve their strategies;

- using the information gained from assessment whether at the start of a topic, at the end, or mid-way through to plan mathematics;

- meeting with other teachers at the school to asses and discuss pupils' work; and

- ensuring that systems for recording assessment information meet teachers' planning and reporting needs, and are easily understood, without becoming too time-consuming to maintain.

135 This part of our report has been well received. We are concerned that all assessment should be purposeful, manageable and informative, and that the training for all schools should be designed to support this objective. Pupils need to be well informed about their strengths and weaknesses and, wherever practical, assessment procedures should involve the pupils themselves. It is important that teachers spend time with pupils discussing their progress in mathematics. Talking to individuals, pairs or small groups of pupils each term allows teachers and pupils alike to review progress and set new goals. This approach motivates pupils to take an active role in their development by judging their own progress and recognising their success over time.

136 The emphasis in our strategy on daily opportunities for oral and mental work has implications for assessment. Regular monitoring of these skills and informal tests of recall and mental calculation are an essential part of the assessment procedures teachers should use to gather the information they need to plan oral and mental work. It is important that these tests build on early successes and promote the knowledge and skills that pupils may have recently acquired. There should also be discussion of mistakes and the different methods used by pupils to reach an answer. This constructive approach is useful for teaching the most effective methods, and also helps to reassure pupils who may be anxious about being tested.

137 As we stated clearly in our preliminary report, none of the planning of these mental tasks and other assessments should be too burdensome. We believe that the examples set out in the *Framework for teaching* will be helpful to teachers, and there is also an increasing range of assessment tools available nationally. Statutory and optional tests, matched to the National Curriculum, are now available for use by schools covering years 2 to 6. The statutory tests at the end of Key Stage 2 now also incorporate mental arithmetic, which we have supported as an essential element of numeracy skills. These tests provide the basis for tracking pupils' progress in numeracy throughout Key Stage 2 and, as stated in our preliminary report, the tests as a whole should be kept under review by QCA to ensure that they provide a fair, consistent picture over time of national progress towards the 2002 numeracy target.

138 Reports on national standards are published annually by QCA for each of the Key Stages 1 to 3. These reports detail pupils' strengths and weaknesses in their answers to the National Curriculum tests and the implications for teaching and learning. We identified these in our preliminary report as a useful tool for helping teachers to plan for improvements in numeracy skills. The reports provide an increasingly longitudinal perspective on pupils' performance in mathematics, and we are keen to encourage their effective use by schools. Other materials exemplifying standards of work, such as those published nationally by QCA and locally by LEAs, also have an important role to play in developing teachers' assessment skills and a common understanding of attainment levels. QCA is developing new materials to help teachers assess children's progress in numeracy by exemplifying the expected standards for pupils in each primary year. It would be helpful for teachers if this guidance could be specifically related to the teaching objectives in the Framework, and, like the guidance on mental calculation strategies, presented to schools as part of a set of documents that will help them implement the numeracy strategy.

139 QCA have commissioned NFER at the DfEE's request to develop criteria for target setting for pupils with SEN in both mainstream and special schools. The scales for targets have detailed descriptions leading to level 1, and between levels 1 and 2, and 2 and 3.

140 The development of teachers' skills in assessment is vital if best use is to be made of the materials and performance information now available. The Task Force believes that schools and LEAs should make innovative use of development funding, such as the Standards Fund, to help with this task. The effective training of teachers in assessment methods and interpretation of results is now a requirement of the ITT National Curriculum.

Classroom resources

141 There was agreement amongst those responding to consultation that there was not as great a need for books and materials to support the implementation of the National Numeracy Strategy as there had been for books to support the introduction of the daily literacy hour. As noted in the previous chapter, the Task Force does not recommend that the numeracy strategy should replicate the average of £1,000 per school for resources funded through the Standards Fund for the National Literacy Strategy. Most schools should already have the basic resources needed to teach the daily mathematics lesson, but we recognise that some of the schools that will have the biggest improvements to make may have an immediate need for resources. Our priority in our proposed allocation of funding has been to maximise the support for release time for training and other direct support. We therefore propose that a limited sum only should be made available for classroom resources in the first year of the strategy, which should be given to LEAs to delegate to those schools that are most poorly equipped in resources for mathematics, following an audit of their provision. We assume that these will typically be the 10 to 15 per cent of schools in the LEA that require intensive support. The training and demonstration lessons we recommend will show teachers how to make the most effective use of essential classroom resources to promote pupils' numeracy skills.

142 The Task Force believes, based on the evidence of successful mathematics teaching in the NNP and other projects, that the following resources would be essential for the daily mathematics lesson:

- a board, flip chart or OHP for demonstrations;

- a variety of large and small number lines and number squares, for display on the wall, below the board for demonstrations, and for use at desks;

- digit cards for individual pupils to use;

- materials for pupils, such as text books of activities and exercises, homework activity sheets and books;

- dice, coins, measuring equipment and other materials to support numeracy skills, such as interlocking cubes; and

- a basic calculator each for older pupils.

143 Others that are desirable include:

- a range of number games and puzzles; and

- an OHP calculator.

144 A good chalkboard or other board for demonstrating is essential for successful whole class teaching. This board needs to be in a position where all the children can easily see it, and where they can easily get to it and reach it to demonstrate their calculations. Members of the Task Force were impressed with the way in which children could use chalkboards, in particular, which they saw on a visit to observe mathematics teaching in Holland, where boards fold inwards and can be raised or lowered for the teacher or child. Use of boards generally has somewhat declined in primary schools in this country. In some classrooms, there is no board at all, and in some it is in poor condition, or difficult to see and use. Where this is the case, we believe that schools should take steps to provide new boards, or improve or reposition the boards that they already have. This is not simply a matter of successful implementation of the National Numeracy Strategy - a board for demonstrations is, after all, useful for many other subjects besides mathematics.

145 LEAs should take into account the needs of special schools when delegating funding for classroom resources, and in carrying out their audit, mainstream primary schools should take account of resources for pupils with special educational needs. Specific resources may be needed to enable the daily mathematics lesson to be accessed by pupils who have particular special needs. For example, textbooks and activity sheets may need to be adapted so that they contain less information on each page. Symbol-supported material would be needed for some pupils, and using tactile dice, calculators and other mathematical equipment, or adapted games and puzzles, would help to increase children's access to, and enjoyment of, mathematics.

Information and Communications Technologies (ICT)

146 There was some concern that *Numeracy Matters* did not say enough about the way in which ICT can support the successful teaching and learning of mathematics. We feel it is important to stress in this context that whilst we see increasing benefits from the use of ICT to support mathematics, we are convinced that ICT must supplement, and cannot replace, an effective teacher. The whole thrust of our recommendations has been to ensure that all teachers are equipped with the knowledge and skills that they need to teach mathematics successfully, and this has been our priority in recommending how the money available for specific support over the years of the National Numeracy Strategy should be spent. We have, therefore, not had sufficient time or opportunity to study the use of ICT in mathematics in depth, and do not give detailed guidance in this report, although we do recognise the potential promise in this area.

147 Our broad priorities in relation to ICT are for teachers to have reliable information on the usefulness for mathematics teaching of the new materials available through technology, and to be able to use the technology effectively to enhance children's learning. We recognise that ICT will have an increasingly important role to play in all subjects, and also acknowledge the potential of existing initiatives to help to realise our aims for ICT in mathematics. The following types of software are especially valuable:

> - software that teachers can use to introduce and develop specific aspects of number, to sharpen pupils' mental recall and calculation skills;
>
> - software that teachers can use for demonstrations with large groups, for example, to zoom in and out of a number line, or to represent data in graphs and charts;
>
> - software that individual children can use to practise and extend what they have been taught in class, which can be used at breaks and lunchtimes by children who need to catch up; and
>
> - programs that give opportunities for children to practise recall of multiplication tables and other number facts in enjoyable ways, which can be useful for children to use at home.

148 The National Council for Educational Technology (NCET) - now the British Educational Communications and Technology Agency (BECTA) - has completed its review of the range and quality of such software noted in our preliminary report. Summaries of the findings have been published and made available to suppliers of educational software in the commercial sector. We note that the DfEE now intends, as recommended in our report, to follow up this assessment in order to create a dialogue between educators and the commercial suppliers to improve the range and quality of materials available to schools in the future.

149 The National Grid for Learning is now being developed in prototype, with a key aim of encouraging continuing improvements in classroom practice. It will include the Virtual Teachers' Centre, and the Standards and Effectiveness Database, as sources of practical advice for teachers. The Lottery-funded ICT training strategy for serving teachers being developed by the Department of Culture, Media and Sport (DCMS), DfEE and TTA is due to commence in 1999. The role of ICT in supporting the teaching of mathematics will be an important aspect of the training, to ensure that it supports the National Numeracy Strategy.

150 We note that BECTA's evaluation of Integrated Learning Systems (ILS) has now been published. ILS could also prove a powerful tool for future classroom teachers. But design of software continues to evolve and understanding in the education system of how to use the systems effectively is still not fully developed. We do not believe that ILS should be seen as systems that offer self-contained solutions, but rather as ones that need to be carefully integrated by teachers. Whatever the potential promise of ILS may be in the medium to long term, it is important that schools look carefully at the evaluation evidence when making a commitment to this form of learning.

Additional adults in the classroom

151 In our preliminary report, we welcomed the contribution that additional adults in the classroom can make in helping teachers to develop children's numeracy skills. We stressed, however, that it was important for these adults to be clear about the strategy, teaching objectives and mathematical terminology, and to work in partnership with the teacher. We recommended that training for specialist teacher assistants (STAs) should form a part of the National Numeracy Strategy. We continue to believe that this is important, but are also convinced that the first priority for the strategy should be to train teachers themselves to teach the daily mathematics lesson. Training for new STAs should be provided as funds allow, but certainly no later than the second year of the strategy. It will, however, be essential to the success of the strategy to ensure that existing adult helpers in schools are well informed about the National Numeracy Strategy. An important role of adults supporting teachers in the daily mathematics lesson is to ensure that the children they are overseeing interpret instructions correctly, concentrate and behave responsibly. Another important part of their role is to question children in ways suggested by the teacher to help develop children's thinking, to practise mathematical vocabulary the teacher has identified during the lesson, and, during oral work with the whole class, give discreet help to children who need it in order to play a full part in the session.

152 If adult helpers are to fulfil their roles effectively, they need to be involved in lesson planning and be properly briefed about their task. Schools should therefore ensure that classroom assistants and other adults receive copies of relevant parts of the *Framework for teaching*. Adult helpers should certainly be included in the INSET sessions for whole school training. The sessions that will be of particular interest are those on the use of classroom resources, on children's common problems and misconceptions, and on practising mental skills in enjoyable and varied ways. Schools should also ensure that their adult helpers are aware of any relevant local training offered through the STA scheme.

Early Years

153 Many of those responding to consultation said that the preliminary report had not given sufficient attention to the needs of Early Years children. The Task Force fully recognises this, and has now given more attention to this issue, taking into account responses to consultation, including helpful advice from the Early Childhood Mathematics Group. The teaching approach we have outlined for Key Stages 1 and 2, particularly the focus on oral and mental work, should promote improved standards in mathematics for children of statutory school age and older. By Early Years, we mean those children who are being educated in pre-schools, nurseries or Reception classes.

154 It is clear that early learning can have a lasting and beneficial effect on children's later development. One of its most important purposes is to prepare children to learn when they enter primary school. This means developing social skills, confidence, memorisation skills and powers of concentration. All providers of pre-school education forming part of a local Early Years Development Plan must ensure that their curriculum allows children to progress towards the Desirable Learning Outcomes. A key part of OFSTED inspection is to judge how effectively the provision will result in the Desirable Outcomes being met. The Task Force is broadly content that the current version of the Desirable Outcomes for mathematics provides a solid foundation for later mathematics achievement in primary school. The current version is as follows:

> "Children use mathematical language, such as "circle", "in front of", "bigger than" and "more" to describe shape, position, size and quantity. They recognise and recreate patterns. They are familiar with number rhymes, songs, stories, counting games and activities. They compare, sort, match, order, sequence and count using everyday objects. They recognise and use numbers to 10 and are familiar with larger numbers from their everyday lives. They begin to use their developing mathematical understanding to solve practical problems. Through practical activities, children understand and record numbers, begin to show awareness of number operations such as addition and subtraction, and begin to use the language involved."

155 We are aware that QCA will be conducting a review of the Desirable Outcomes at the same time as the National Curriculum. We do not think that the range of the Outcomes should be greatly narrowed, as the emphasis on social and broader learning skills is important for preparing children to learn in a school setting, in mathematics and other subjects. These skills are especially important if children are to be taught in a whole class for much of the time, and in smaller groups for specific purposes, when they move into Year 1. We believe it would be helpful, however, for QCA, to clarify in the review the relationship between personal and social skills, and the specific skills in the Desirable Learning Outcomes for mathematics, which will best prepare children for later education.

156 Our recommended strategy envisages that children would be taught together as a whole class right from the beginning of Year 1, and for some of the time in Reception. Baseline assessment is intended to identify each child's needs on entry to primary school, so that education can be provided that meets those needs. It is quite possible to accommodate a range of attainment at this stage, with children learning about mathematical ideas and language through a broad range of stimulating, interactive activities. The experience of the NNP has been that children who know less about mathematics than others when they enter a Reception class can derive great benefit, and make considerable progress, by listening to, and watching, their peers engage in mathematical activities for part of their time. This is an important stage of learning, which gradually allows them to participate successfully in the activities.

157 Our strategy aims to raise the standards of mathematics for all pupils in a class, with differentiation to that end, to ensure as far as possible that all children reach an acceptable level for their age. In the same way, all children in pre-school education should have an equal opportunity to make the maximum possible progress towards the Desirable Learning Outcomes. Where there are large gaps between children's attainment at the time of baseline assessment in mathematics, the outcomes of the assessment should be used to give extra time and support to those children, to ensure that the gaps are made smaller.

158 It is important to stress that the Desirable Learning Outcomes for mathematics should not be interpreted in a way that places too great an emphasis on formal recording of written numerals and calculations. The emphasis, particularly in the very early years, should be to learn about mathematical ideas through counting activities and discussions that enable children to become familiar with numbers and numerals and use these to solve number problems in a practical context.

159 The most important experience that pre-school education can give is to prepare children for learning, in particular, training them to listen closely, to concentrate for reasonable periods, to respond quickly, to sit still when necessary and to value the contributions of other children. There should be stimulating, interactive, sessions in groups, and with the whole class being taught together. These sessions can be used to focus on memory games, songs, counting activities, and oral and practical addition and subtraction. This type of teaching will make a real difference to the children's ability to flourish in the whole class teaching of mathematics that we recommend as a central feature of the National Numeracy Strategy.

Secondary schools

The impact of the strategy on secondary schools

160 There was unanimous agreement amongst those responding to consultation that the Task Force's recommendations would inevitably have an impact on the curriculum and teaching of mathematics in secondary schools. It was agreed that the National Numeracy Strategy would need to include measures for secondary schools in order to support and develop the strategy and raise standards. Many respondents drew attention to the needs of pupils currently entering secondary school with low attainment in mathematics. These pupils will need extra support with basic numeracy skills in order to function successfully in secondary school and later in life. Over time, the National Numeracy Strategy should make far-reaching improvements in mathematics in primary schools, so that the great majority of pupils enter secondary schools with the essential numeracy skills they need to cope with the demands they will face.

161 The Task Force recognises that numeracy skills are important at all levels of mathematics, and in other subject disciplines such as science, geography and economics, up to A level and beyond. We believe it is essential that the momentum of change in primary schools, and special schools for primary aged children, is not lost at higher levels, but that secondary schools continue to build up their pupils' skills. It is important that teachers in secondary schools and in middle schools understand the National Numeracy Strategy and the impact it will have on teaching in schools. In particular, they should be familiar with the *Framework for teaching*, and we recommend that every secondary school receives at least one copy of it.

162 We believe that secondary schools would welcome some extra help to prepare for the first influx of pupils who will have experienced the daily mathematics lesson in primary schools based on the practices we recommend for the National Numeracy Strategy, in the autumn term of 2000. This can be done by providing conferences for heads of mathematics departments in secondary schools in the summer term of 2000, to explore the implementation of the strategy in primary schools in more detail and its impact on teaching and standards in secondary schools. We strongly recommend that secondary schools should start planning for this intake as soon as practicable. Once the head of mathematics is familiar with the strategy, including the *Framework for teaching*, he or she could lead a training day in 1999/2000 to consider with colleagues the implications for the teaching of mathematics and other disciplines. In LEAs where there are well established links between secondary schools and their feeder primary schools, preparation could include arranged visits to primary schools to see the strategy brought to life, or participating in cluster meetings. LEA advisers will have a key role to play in supporting and encouraging these cross-phase links, and in preparing secondary schools to consolidate and further improve the skills pupils will have developed in primary schools. LEAs will need to consider how they can best influence practice and help to raise standards in mathematics and other disciplines in secondary schools.

Developing numeracy skills at Key Stage 3

163   We recommended in our preliminary report that secondary mathematics teachers should ensure that pupils' mental calculation strategies are fully developed in Key Stage 3. A secure foundation of oral and mental work is essential if pupils are to continue to develop their mathematical skills. The Task Force recognises the valuable support that teachers in secondary schools already provide for pupils with poor numeracy skills. We believe that the current work should be continued and extended. If mathematics teachers in secondary schools do not already have effective strategies for helping Key Stage 3 pupils with poor numeracy skills to catch up with their peers, they should use the Framework as a tool to help them plan action to improve these pupils' mental calculation skills, focusing particularly on the recall of facts and calculation strategies identified in the Framework. This extra teaching could be given to pupils within a school's existing timetabled time for mathematics, in a few 5 to 10 minute slots each week. It could also be in 'add on' programmes at lunch time for example.

164   The Task Force's main aim has been, understandably, to improve the skills of pupils who are not achieving high enough standards. We are also aware, however, that many pupils will leave primary school with attainment at or above Level 4, the level expected for their age, and that this proportion will increase as the strategy continues and develops. It is essential that these pupils continue to progress and to acquire higher order numeracy skills. For many of these pupils, the opportunity to apply numeracy skills in order to solve increasingly complex problems will present them with the challenges they need in order to keep their skills sharp, and acquire new techniques by using these skills in new contexts.

165   The Task Force believes that a small proportion of the funding available for the strategy in 1999-2000 should be used to support pilot projects that build on the needs of pupils in this age group, and the good work already being done in this area by the Basic Skills Agency and others. These projects should involve groups of secondary schools and, where appropriate, middle schools, with a high proportion of pupils who are attaining low standards at Key Stage 3. The projects should provide intensive support programmes targeted at pupils who attain Level 3 or below in mathematics at the end of Key Stage 2 using, where appropriate, the approaches to mathematics teaching we recommend in

this report for primary schools, together with the *Framework for teaching* and QCA's guidance on mental calculation. As such, the projects supported should:

- identify a time when pupils are to receive the intensive support in numeracy, whether within a mathematics lesson or outside normal lesson time;

- set clear learning objectives and targets;

- promote pupils' oral and mental recall and calculation skills;

- ensure that pupils' numeracy skills are regularly assessed, to inform pupils, teachers and parents about the progress they are making;

- set activities that pupils can do at home or in study support centres;

- engage teachers from different departments in supporting the programme in their teaching of their own subjects; and

- strengthen links with primary feeder schools, sharing teaching programmes, standards achieved in the feeder school, and other assessment information.

166 We also believe that to support secondary teachers' expertise in maintaining progression and continuity in the teaching of mathematics, it would be helpful for the DfEE's revision of the Framework to include extension into Key Stage 3 . The TTA should consider whether it would be appropriate to develop needs assessment materials in mathematics for non-specialist teachers in Key Stage 3.

Transition from Key Stage 2 to Key Stage 3

167 It is clear that the quality of transition between primary and secondary school has a major effect on the success of pupils at all levels of attainment in maintaining and improving their skills in all subjects. This transition is certainly a significant event in pupils' lives, but inspection and research evidence shows that for too many this "new start" is all too often a "start again". Secondary schools can often repeat unnecessarily work that has already been grasped. Familiarity with the National Numeracy Strategy, including the Framework, should help to improve continuity in future, and secondary schools should take account of the standards pupils have already achieved, and seek to give them as many opportunities as possible to tackle problems that develop and extend the numeracy skills the strategy seeks to promote. Problem solving is one example of a good vehicle for whole class discussion, and for oral and mental work, which can, if done well, challenge pupils of all abilities. The Task Force notes that the ITT National Curriculum for secondary mathematics emphasises effective progress for pupils from primary to secondary school phase. We welcome the fact that trainee teachers on 11-16 and 11-18 courses will have to be taught about progression in mathematics from Key Stage 2, and in particular to teach mental strategies building on those taught at primary level, and to identify effective strategies for teaching pupils whose attainment in mathematics is below that expected for their age.

168 More generally, secondary schools need to receive, and act upon, high quality information about the mathematical knowledge and skills that pupils bring with them from their primary schools. The information available is improving, as is the use made of it by teachers, but more needs to be done to ensure that teachers' expectations match pupils' attainment when they enter secondary school. We welcome the further work that QCA has in hand to improve the quality, consistency and flow of information, and believe that schools and LEAs themselves should continue to work at such improvements. It would be helpful if secondary schools identified a mathematics teacher concerned with liaison with primary schools, who could also attend the conferences for secondary heads of mathematics.

169 We are pleased that Ministers have already acted upon our recommendation to run a pilot programme of summer numeracy schools, building on the lessons learnt in last year's pilot of summer literacy schools. A pilot programme of at least 50 schools will run this summer, to explore good practice in LEAs involved in projects to raise standards of primary mathematics, including the NNP. The Task Force was consulted during the production of bidding guidance, and successful bids were announced in June. It will be important for the evaluation of this pilot to explore ways of improving the transition between Key Stages 2 and 3.

Recommendations

DfEE should:

autumn term 1998

- consider the scope for including an element of STA training in funding for the National Numeracy Strategy, at the latest for 2000-2001;

- invite bids from LEAs to run pilot programmes for improving and extending numeracy skills at Key Stage 3; and

- continue to develop and expand the database of good practice and materials on the National Grid for Learning, to support effective teaching of mathematics.

spring term 1999

- ensure that the guidance, training and support for the strategy helps teachers to teach the daily mathematics lesson to classes with a high proportion of pupils with SEN, EAL pupils, in small schools and with exceptionally able pupils; and

- start to develop the *Framework for teaching* to Year 7, working closely with QCA.

spring term 2000

- prepare and distribute guidelines and training materials for LEAs about conferences for secondary heads of mathematics.

summer term 2000

- fund conferences for secondary heads of mathematics and those in charge of primary liaison to prepare them for the first intake of pupils from primary schools to have experienced the numeracy strategy.

QCA should:

autumn term 1998

- ensure that the revised National Curriculum for mathematics emphasises oral and mental work in Key Stages 1 and 2, and that formal written work builds upon these secure foundations;

- take account of the structure and approach of the revised *Framework for teaching* when making changes to the National Curriculum for mathematics, so that it is easy for teachers to see how the Framework is used to plan, and teach, the curriculum requirements; and

- in the review of the Desirable Learning Outcomes, seek to make more explicit the relative emphasis to be given to personal and social skills, and the specific skills needed in mathematics.

spring term 1999

- publish guidance on mental calculation strategies and on how calculators can be most effectively and sensibly used, that is specifically related to the revised *Framework for teaching*;

- publish exemplification material to help teachers monitor pupils' progress towards the teaching objectives in the Framework for Numeracy; and

- prepare advice on written calculation, which would usefully be included with the distance learning materials to be distributed to schools in summer 1999.

LEAs should:

summer 1998

- work with schools to make continuous improvements to the arrangements for transfer of pupils between primary and secondary schools.

summer term 1999

- delegate funds to schools to spend on classroom resources for mathematics, in accordance with their audited needs.

summer term 2000

- run conferences about the strategy for secondary heads of mathematics.

Primary and middle schools, and where appropriate, special schools, should:

spring term 1999

- begin to familiarise themselves with the National Numeracy Strategy including the *Framework for teaching mathematics*, and QCA exemplification materials and guidance on the development of mental calculation strategies.

summer term 1999

- particularly where the school has a high proportion of children with SEN, send the SENCO to the initial 3 day training course with the headteacher, mathematics co-ordinator and governor;

- involve adult helpers fully in preparation and training for the implementation of the National Numeracy Strategy;

- prepare medium term teaching plans for the autumn term and beyond, based on the yearly teaching programmes in the Framework; and

- prepare for, and start to use, the distance learning materials and QCA guidance on mental calculation.

autumn term 1999

- begin to teach the daily mathematics lesson for all pupils of between 45 minutes and one hour, depending on children's ages, in line with the recommended structure;

- ensure that suitable assessment procedures are in place to inform everyday teaching; and

- provide where possible and practical the time and opportunity for the SENCO to work with the mathematics co-ordinator and other colleagues to implement the strategy within the school.

Mathematics teachers in secondary schools should:

spring term 1999

- familiarise themselves with the National Numeracy Strategy, including the structure and requirements of the *Framework for teaching*.

autumn term 1999

- plan and provide recovery programmes for Key Stage 3 pupils who have attained level 3 or below at Key Stage 2, focusing on mental calculation skills and strategies based on the *Framework for teaching*.

summer term 2000

- send representatives to attend conferences about the National Numeracy Strategy to prepare for the first intake of pupils to have been taught the daily mathematics lesson in line with the *Framework*.

autumn term 2000

- receive, and begin to teach, the first intake of Year 7 pupils who have experienced the National Numeracy Strategy.

TTA should:

autumn term 1998

- consider the possibility of needs assessment material for non-specialist mathematics teachers at Key Stage 3.

 # Creating a climate of support at home and in the wider community

The importance of support

170 A very high proportion of those responding to consultation welcomed the recognition given by the Task Force to the importance of the influence of parents and the wider community on children's educational achievements generally and in mathematics in particular. There was wide acceptance of the principle that both parents and society at large could help to show children the importance and practical benefit of numeracy skills. People generally agreed with the Task Force's view that these skills tend to be undervalued in comparison to literacy skills, and that this would have to be changed if standards were to be raised.

171 The National Year of Reading, which will run from September 1998, was explicitly intended by the Literacy Task Force to back up teachers' efforts to raise standards in the classroom, by ensuring that children got positive messages and role models for reading outside it. The Numeracy Task Force, too, would like to see public attitudes to numeracy change for the better, so that teachers who are trying to raise standards feel they are swimming with the tide of public opinion. Our expanded proposals for the World Mathematical Year 2000 later in the chapter seek to do this. The first part of the chapter, however, is concerned with the first, and probably most important, influence on children - their parents.

Parents' involvement in their children's education

172 It is clear from responses to consultation that involving parents in numeracy is seen as an important part of the strategy. It is equally clear that parents need to be well-informed about what their children are learning, and confident about the activities they are doing with their children, if their involvement is to be helpful. This means that involving parents means much more than just encouraging them to support their children in doing homework, though this is an important aspect.

173 It means that schools need to work in an active partnership with children's parents or other carers in a way that bridges the gap between home and school. This does not need to take up too much time, and should be enjoyable and rewarding for parents, children and teachers alike. Schools need to give careful thought to the best way of involving parents and carers in their children's learning - some will need more encouragement and support than others. A few may be almost too eager to impose their own way of doing things. It is important to strike a balance. The Task Force has given thought, taking into account the responses to consultation, to the kind of mathematical activities to promote numeracy skills that might best achieve this balance.

Parents and numeracy

174 As stated in the preliminary report, almost all parents are much more uncertain about how to help their children with numeracy skills than they are about reading with their children. Everyone seemed to agree with that. It is therefore all the more important to find ways of involving parents that build their confidence and give them practical and accurate information about their child's learning. We made clear in our preliminary report that parents are almost certainly already doing, and talking about, many things with their children that can be exploited to improve numeracy skills. Going shopping and counting out change, telling the time, spotting properties of bus and car numbers, even deciding which television programme to watch and setting the video recorder, are all examples of this. But these can be exploited all the more if parents are aware of the potential these activities have, and have some concept of how they relate to the numeracy activities that their children are doing at school. Above all, helping their children in this way need not be difficult, and there is good deal that the school can do to reassure parents about this.

175 It is obviously helpful for schools to send information home about what children of different ages should know, understand and be able to do, or booklets of practical activities that can be done as part of homework. But many respondents to consultation mentioned the effectiveness of bringing parents into the school, as well as sending material home. The Task Force believes that open evenings or other informal meetings to explain to parents the methods being used to teach mathematics can be extremely valuable. Parents can often be worried or confused about helping their children because they think that the methods being used to teach mathematics now are different from when they were at school. These events can play a major part in dispelling parents' worries, and making them realise that you do not have to be "good at maths" to help your children. They should not just involve one way communication from the school to parents, but should actively engage parents in enjoyable mathematical activities. Parents and children can attend the events together, and children can have the chance to "teach" their parents the sort of activities they do in their mathematics lessons. For example, parents can split into groups to do practical mathematics activities that illustrate the points being made, then come together again to discuss what they have done.

176 It is also important for parents to feel that teachers are available on a continuing basis to discuss particular aspects of their child's learning with them, or clear up worries or things they do not understand. Possible strategies include devoting a specific day in the week, or every fortnight, to problems with mathematics or an occasional "helpline" on a particular evening of term, for parents who would find it difficult to get to the school. We recognise, however, that many of the parents the school most needs to reach will be unlikely to attend on a specific evening, and even more may be put off by any event with "mathematics" in its title. It may be best in these cases to address individual invitations to parents, which they are less likely to turn down.

177 There is a wide range of quite simple things that schools can do, in addition to events like these, to engage parents in developing their children's numeracy skills, many of them tried and tested with a variety of families in the NNP and the Hamilton Maths Project. These include:

> ● organising "film shows" of video film or slides of their children at work on mathematics in class;
>
> ● sharing with parents the expectations for what most children in each year group should know, understand and be able to do;
>
> ● keeping a library of mathematical games, puzzles and other equipment for parents to borrow parents who have the time might be encouraged to help

make the games or to run the games library, not least because parents who are reluctant to get involved with school can often feel more encouraged to use this service if it is offered by another parent rather than a teacher;

- inviting parents to work with children at mathematics in school;

- inviting parents to help with lunch-time or after school clubs with a focus on mathematics, such as outdoor number games (e.g. hopscotch, quoits) or indoor games (e.g. dominoes, snakes and ladders);

- planning a "maths trail" in the school grounds or local area, which parents and children can walk together, pointing out interesting mathematical features; and

- inviting parents to a "maths assembly", at which children sing songs and say rhymes with a number focus, and show some of their mathematical work.

178 The Task Force hopes that all primary and special schools will follow these examples, and invent activities of their own. We are also aware, however, that not all parents will share the same enthusiasm for getting involved, however hard schools try to take steps to make activities and events attractive and relevant to them. Some parents will be overburdened with other work and family commitments, and some will simply be unwilling to make contact with the school at all. For the latter group in particular, it is important for information about learning to come to the places where they regularly go, so that they can pick it up easily and, ideally, come to realise that their children's education is a part of their everyday lives. It is for this reason that the Task Force's preliminary report recommended producing leaflets that could be made available in supermarkets, explaining primary mathematics to parents and how they can help their children to develop numeracy skills. We continue to believe that such leaflets have a valuable role to play. They should, ideally, be placed in as many different outlets as possible, including doctors' surgeries, video shops, public libraries and pubs.

Homework and working at home

179 Formal homework, and informal working at home on numeracy activities, are both key ways in which the gap between home and school can be bridged, and parents can make a real contribution to their children's progress. Neither activity means pages of "sums" for parents to check, but a variety of activities that children can do outside lesson time, to reinforce and extend their numeracy skills. The activities and information referred to in the previous section should help to ensure that parents' support is used in effective and enjoyable ways for parent and child alike. In particular, we believe that homework has an important part to play in any strategy to improve standards of numeracy. The training we have proposed for schools needing intensive support includes a session on the use of homework activities. The training and other support materials for the strategy should also include guidance for schools, with practical examples of good practice, to show the sort of homework that will support the acquisition of numeracy skills. Further examples of good practice could be included on the National Grid for Learning.

180 The Task Force would like to emphasise the following three principles, in particular, which we believe should underpin this aspect of the National Numeracy Strategy, and are consistent with the draft homework guidelines:

● **Making sure that homework is appropriate to children's ages and supports progression in their learning at school.** The nature and purpose of homework will vary according to children's ages and, correspondingly, parents' role in supporting it. For younger children, the focus will be on activities that parents and children can do together, which need not take up much time. Research has shown that parental involvement and interest in the activities for young children is possibly more important than the activities themselves. Older children at primary school will, from time to time, have more formal number exercises as well as less formal activities, but their parents can still have some involvement in these. This need not be intimidating for parents - after all, one of the most useful ways of getting a child to learn calculation skills is to explain to someone else how they have done a particular calculation. As pupils get older, there should be an increasing emphasis in homework on developing children's skills of working independently, but children of all ages still need the interest and encouragement of their parents. In all cases, the homework or other home activity should help to consolidate and reinforce pupils' skills and understanding in mathematics, in a way that helps them to make progress in class.

● **Showing that the school values what is done at home.** It is important that both parents and children understand that schools value their efforts in respect of homework, and see this as an important part of learning. Children need feedback from their teachers as well as their parents on what they have done, which means that teachers need to plan time for feedback, including prompt marking of homework where appropriate, so that it forms an integral part of teaching and learning. The Hamilton Maths Project and the NNP have promoted the use of homework diaries to allow parents to give concise, direct feedback to teachers about how different activities went, and for the teachers, in turn, to respond to the parents. It is also sometimes possible for the teacher to go through homework exercises with the whole class, and for the children to mark their own or each other's work. This can be particularly effective with younger pupils. A relatively simple gesture, such as displaying mathematical work done at home near the entrance to the school, can help to show parents how their input is seen as a useful extension of what is done in class.

> ● **Ensuring that all pupils have adequate homework opportunities.** The Task Force welcomes the existing opportunities provided by schools and others for study support and the DfEE's plans to expand these, as a means of giving all children access to suitable facilities and help to do homework - especially important where parents are unable to take an active interest. We hope that the scope that the study support offers will be exploited to improve numeracy skills. It is also important that facilities for after-school care of children are properly equipped for them to do homework and, particularly for younger children, that the staff of these facilities are confident and knowledgeable about participating with the children in mathematical activities.

181 The Basic Skills Agency magazine, *Count and Figure It Out Together*, was mentioned in the Task Force's preliminary report. This is designed for the parents of 3 to 5 year olds and has been enthusiastically received in LEAs and schools. A publication of this sort could provide a continuing bank of ideas for activities for parents to do at home with young children. We also note that the Basic Skills Agency plans to launch a national parents' information line, following a regional pilot, giving advice to parents about ways they can support their children's literacy and numeracy skills. Schools should help to make parents aware of this service.

Education Action Zones (EAZs)

182 The Task Force believes that EAZs may well be potentially valuable in creating opportunities for parents, children and the community to work together in innovative ways to improve numeracy skills outside the normal school day and environment. Their focus on disadvantaged areas means that they are likely to be particularly useful for drawing in families who might not normally be willing to participate in this kind of activity. We therefore hope that a number of pilot EAZs will be chosen that explicitly include a focus on numeracy, by building on existing community links, using local further and higher education institutions to improve the numeracy skills of adults, and promoting the importance and enjoyment of numeracy skills through local media and business.

Improving parents' numeracy skills

183 Many responses to consultation that mentioned parents also noted that some parents were likely to feel that their own numeracy skills needed improving as well as their children's. The incentive of playing the active role in their children's learning that this chapter envisages should prove to be powerful encouragement.

184 We have been interested in the information the Basic Skills Agency has provided for the Task Force about their Family Numeracy pilot programme. This has involved over 500 families in 14 LEAs. Most of the parents involved had poor levels of qualifications, and were not employed outside the home. More than half of the parents involved with the pilot now have significantly more contact with their children's schools, and more than half have significantly improved their own mathematical skills and knowledge. It is also evident that the families who took part in the pilot now do far more numeracy-related activities at home, of a higher quality than before. We are very pleased to learn of the effect that the programme has had on children's levels of achievement in mathematics, and it appears to be an effective early intervention to help children at risk of poor attainment in mathematics. Most of the children who took part in the pilot were between 3 and 6 years old, and made significantly more progress in their achievement in number and awareness of mathematical language than children who had not taken part.

185 The Task Force recommends that the pilot programme be developed and extended as part of the National Numeracy Strategy. It will be important to ensure that the programme continues to provide an effective means of improving the skills of parents and children alike, whilst obtaining good value for money. We are particularly keen that the activities forming part of the programme should closely link to the activities in mathematics at their schools.

World Mathematical Year 2000

186 Virtually all respondents welcomed the idea of giving an educational slant to the World Mathematical Year 2000, being led by UNESCO. There was some concern that the year might be too esoteric and that activities would need to be designed that emphasised the fun and practical value of numeracy skills and which were designed to appeal to children and involve families. As noted earlier in this chapter, it will be important to include in the Year activities that help to draw in parents from socio-economic groups, who might otherwise not want to get involved with developing their children's numeracy skills. This means using unexpected people, places and experiences to promote and develop numeracy skills. This will be a challenge, but achievable with help from a range of partners. It will be important to define the Year's objectives clearly. The Year should certainly be linked to the Millennium celebrations being planned by government and many others, which will help to raise its profile and popular appeal.

187 The Task Force is keen that the DfEE should take up this challenge, building on the experience it had already gained in the run-up to the National Year of Reading. This planning will have put the Department in touch with a wide range of organisations that might not automatically get involved with educational activities, such as the media, business and a wide range of voluntary organisations. We would urge the Department to begin discussions with UNESCO, organisations responsible for the National Year of Reading and other contacts now about how the same goodwill, enthusiasm and expertise can be applied to mathematics. The National Year of Reading is being planned by a network of local planning groups convened by each local authority and involving partnerships across all sectors, including education, health, libraries and local business via TECs and Education Business Partnerships (EBPs). We agree with the philosophy that no national promotional effort will create a lasting change in attitudes and behaviour unless it is backed up with local activities that involve people. These local cross-sector partnerships should, therefore, also be built upon, using the experience of the National Year of Reading, to create a national push for mathematics.

188 With all these points in mind, we have been pleased to have been offered quite a number of new suggestions for specific activities, and offers of help - including some quite unusual ideas. The ideas include:

189 Activities mainly aimed at children

> - putting number puzzles and games on the back of beer mats and place mats in fast food restaurants;
>
> - giving out numeracy stickers for young children at post offices and banks, each with a number fact, so that children collect a set of number facts;
>
> - giving away number games to children: for example, in petrol stations and motorway service stations;
>
> - including material for mathematical games and puzzles in magazines and supermarket magazines for parents to use at home with their children;
>
> - painting more games that can develop numeracy skills, such as snakes and ladders, on the floor of children's play areas in parks;
>
> - encouraging libraries to provide books and videos related to numeracy, and to loan mathematical games to parents;
>
> - putting mathematical puzzles and "amazing mathematical facts" on the back of cereal packets;
>
> - displaying numeracy leaflets in supermarkets with games and puzzles for children to use with their parents while shopping;
>
> - encouraging software developers to produce good quality mathematics software for school and home markets, including CD Roms with interesting ideas and facts about numbers;

- using World Statistical Day as an opportunity to run a children's census on the Internet, giving the results to schools to use as a teaching resource;

- designing a new children's TV or comic character - or adopting an existing one - for children to associate with mathematics during the Year;

- involving the media in developing mathematical quiz shows for children and their parents; and

- using high profile sites to host exhibitions on children's mathematics, with live demonstrations of mathematical skills and interesting problems by celebrities.

190 **Activities to improve the numeracy skills of adults**

- running activities to promote awareness of personal finance skills as essential life skills for present and future adults;

- using storylines in TV soaps to illustrate the problems of poor numeracy skills and what can be done to improve them; and

- developing adults' numeracy skills through workshops in schools.

191 **Activities to encourage interest in mathematics in society at large**

- publicising the quality and variety of career prospects leading from qualifications in mathematics;

- launching a set of commemorative stamps for the World Mathematical Year 2000;

- running a high profile television campaign with celebrities, family games and competitions;

- using the Internet to exchange mathematical ideas with other countries;

- holding community evenings in schools to enable pupils to show the local community what they know about mathematics, and for the whole community, including business, to show how it relates to everyone's daily lives;

- including exhibits within the Millennium Dome and other Millennium exhibitions to allow children and adults to explore mathematical concepts, using puzzles and games;

> - giving a mathematical name to a rose or other flower at the Chelsea flower show, and relating it to numbers in nature;
>
> - giving a mathematical focus to the British Association's public events in 2000; and
>
> - using the media to build on public interest in "popular science" books to promote mathematics.

192 The Task Force recommends that the DfEE follow these and other ideas up as soon as possible so that planning begins in good time. As recommended in our preliminary report, the TTA should also think about ways in which the publicity for mathematics during 2000 could be used to reinforce the recruitment strategy for teachers of mathematics at both primary and secondary levels.

Recommendations

DfEE should:

autumn term 1998

- start planning for the World Mathematical Year 2000, beginning dialogue in particular with key players and local networks in the National Year of Reading; and

- give priority to supporting EAZ bids that put forward creative ideas for engaging the whole community in improving children's standards of numeracy and the numeracy skills of adults, addressing in particular the need for participation from families that have not readily engaged with local schools.

spring term 1999

- include guidance in the training and support materials, on good practice in homework activities to support mathematics for children of different ages and a specific session on homework activities in the training materials developed to support the 5 day course for schools receiving intensive support.

autumn term 1999

- distribute leaflets to supermarkets and similar outlets, developed with QCA and the Basic Skills Agency, building on what the NNP and Hamilton Maths Project have already done, covering:

  - a general introduction to the importance of numeracy and the role parents can play;
  - the sorts of things children should be able to do at the end of each school year; and
  - activities for parents and children appropriate to children's different ages.

- make these leaflets available to after school childcare facilities to ensure that these staff, as well as parents, are fully informed;

- make further guidance on good practice in mathematics homework activities available on the National Grid for Learning; and

- ensure that the investment in study support facilities for all ages takes account of the importance of developing and practising numeracy skills.

Primary schools and, where appropriate, special schools, should:

autumn term 1998

- begin to build up a stock of number games that families can borrow to use at home.

summer term 1999

- when auditing their mathematics provision, consider the extent to which they have suitable books and materials to support mathematics homework.

autumn term 1999

- arrange open evenings and other opportunities to tell parents about the teaching methods they will be using as they implement the National Numeracy Strategy, and how parents can help their children develop good numeracy skills; and

- begin to set regular mathematical activities or exercises for all children to do at home with their parents.

The Basic Skills Agency should:

- continue to publish *Count and Figure It Out Together*, as a continuing resource to support home numeracy activities with younger children, taking into account the objectives for these children in the National Numeracy Strategy; and

- extend the Family Numeracy programme, building on the lessons of the 1998 pilot, aiming for maximum cost effectiveness and links to children's progress in the mainstream school curriculum.

TTA should:

spring term 1999

- consider how the developing plans for World Mathematical Year 2000 can be used to reinforce recruitment strategies for mathematics teachers.

Annex I

National Numeracy Strategy: *Timetable of Key Events*

When?	DfEE	LEAs	Primary and special schools	Secondary schools	Other agencies
summer 1998, and autumn term 1998	• develops the *Framework for teaching* with QCA, TTA, OFSTED and others; • recruits the strategy's National and Regional Directors; • announces successful bids for Summer Numeracy Schools; • informs LEAs of the number of numeracy consultant posts that can be funded from 1 April 1999; • begins work on specification for national training materials; • develops distance learning materials for INSET, including video material; • invites bids from LEAs for Standards Fund support, including LEA numeracy targets for 2002 and local action plans to be agreed by Christmas; • prepares training for consultants and "learning mathematics teachers"; • implements the ITT National Curriculum for primary mathematics; • continues to develop and expand database of good practice in mathematics on National Grid for learning; • invites bids from LEAs to run pilot programmes for numeracy skills at Key Stage 3; and • starts planning for the World Mathematical Year 2000.	• build up clusters and other local networks of schools; • identify prospective "leading mathematics teachers"; • recruit numeracy consultants to take up post from 1 April 1999; and • submit Standards Fund bids and proposed LEA numeracy targets for 2002 to the DfEE.	• familiarise their schools with the National Numeracy Strategy; • schools identify, if they have not already done so, a teacher to act as mathematics coordinator; and • begin to build up a stock of number activities and games that families can borrow to use at home.		• **TTA** ensures that national standards for headteachers, subject leaders and SENCOs take account of their roles in developing numeracy skills; • **QCA** reviews the National Curriculum for primary mathematics, taking account of the revised *Framework for teaching*; • **QCA** reviews the Desirable Outcomes; and • **TTA** begins to consider the possibility of mathematics needs assessment material for Key Stage 3.

When?	DfEE	LEAs	Primary and special schools	Secondary schools	Other agencies
spring term 1999	• early in the term, sends copies of the Framework to primary, special and secondary schools; LEAs and ITT providers; • Regional Directors, train numeracy consultants and "leading mathematics teachers", and run conferences for LEA staff; • with TTA, holds regional conferences for ITT providers; and • prepares training materials for schools.	• negotiate and agree numeracy targets with schools for 2002; • work with Regional Directors on training for consultants and "leading mathematics teachers"; and • identify schools needing intensive support in the first year.	• begin to familiarise themselves with the *Framework for teaching*, and the complementary guidance from QCA.	• mathematics teachers begin to familiarise themselves with the Framework.	• QCA produces guidance on mental calculation strategies, and on exemplification of pupils' standards of achievement, to complement the Framework; • QCA prepares advice on written calculation; • **QCA and Basic skills Agency** work with DfEE to produce leaflets for parents; and • **TTA** begins to consider how World Mathematical Year 2000 can reinforce recruitment strategies.
summer term 1999	• sends distance learning materials to schools to support the three INSET days for the strategy.	• facilitate arrangements for teachers to watch demonstration lessons taught by a consultant or "leading mathematics teacher;" • run 3 day conferences for primary and special schools, supported by DfEE materials; and • delegate funds to some schools for resources, based on an audit of needs.	• the headteacher, mathematics coordinator and another teacher (preferably the SENCO) attend a local 3 day training course, with the governor attending for at least the third day; • all devote one INSET day after the conference, to a whole training event to prepare for the daily mathematics lesson, involving adult helpers; and • audit their current practice in mathematics.		• **Basic Skills Agency** extends the Family Numeracy programme, building on the lessons of the 1998 pilot; • QCA sends guidance to schools on written calculation; and • OFSTED runs training for Inspectors on the National Numeracy Strategy.
autumn term 1999	• distributes leaflets for parents and other carers to a variety of outlets, and to after school childcare facilities; and • implements the ITT National Curriculum for secondary mathematics.		• begin to teach a daily mathematics lesson for all pupils, in line with the strategy's recommended structure; • ensure the SENCO has time to work with colleagues to implement the strategy; and • begin to set regular mathematical activities and exercises for children to do at home.		• OFSTED begins visits to schools to evaluate strategy.

When?	DfEE	LEAs	Primary and special schools	Secondary schools	Other agencies
autumn term 1999 cont'd			• early in the term, all teachers watch at least one demonstration lesson, taught either by a numeracy consultant, a "leading mathematics teacher", the school's mathematics co-ordinator, or on video; • devote a further INSET day to the strategy; • by half term firmly establish the daily mathematics lesson in all classrooms, beginning to allow for the mathematics coordinator to work with colleagues; • begin to arrange open evenings and other opportunities to tell parents about mathematics teaching and how they can help their children; and • mathematics coordinators and another teacher from schools receiving intensive support attend a further course now or later in the year.		
spring term 2000			• devote another INSET day to further training supported by national materials.		
summer term 2000	• Regional Directors run conferences for secondary schools.			• secondary mathematics teachers and those in charge of primary liaison attend conferences about the National Numeracy Strategy.	
autumn term 2000				• receive first intake of pupils to have been taught the strategy's daily mathematics lesson.	

Annex II

Funding the National Numeracy Strategy

Year 1 - 1999-2000	Approx. cost (£m)*

1. LEA numeracy consultants — 14.5
- Employment of up to 300 LEA numeracy consultants and administrative support for their posts

2. Supply cover for all schools — 31
- 3 day training course for headteacher, mathematics co-ordinator and one other teacher, with governor attending for one day
- 5 days extra release time for co-ordinator, or other staff

3. Schools receiving intensive support — 5

The following support for around 10%-15% of schools:
- Supply cover for 5 day training course for mathematics co-ordinator and one other teacher
- Classroom resources for mathematics teaching

4. Key Stage 3 projects — 1
- Small number of promising LEA projects

Total cost — 51.5

Support for LEA numeracy consultants and the Key Stage 3 projects should continue at similar levels in future years. A programme of intensive support should also continue to be provided so that up to 60% of schools receive such support over the first three years of the strategy. It would be possible for about two-thirds of schools receiving intensive support in Year 1 to continue to receive intensive support in Year 2, and some beyond that.

Although the Task Force would expect further release time to be available to all schools in future years, we do not expect the supply cover costs of the 3 day training course for all schools to arise beyond Year 1. This should free up resources to address other priorities, such as a programme of Specialist Teacher Assistant (STA) training, or further funding for classroom resources if these are necessary.

Figures are the Task Force's best estimates of the likely cost of the various elements of the proposed strategy.

Annex III

Recommendations

This annex draws together the recommendations that appear at the end of chapters 2, 3 and 4, as a resource for schools and others who need a comprehensive picture of their part in the strategy.

The DfEE should:

summer 1998

- undertake further development of the *Framework for teaching*, in the light of the input given by senior figures from mathematics associations, and further input from QCA, TTA, and OFSTED;

- begin recruiting national and regional support staff for the National Numeracy Strategy, with the intention of having all these appointed no later than the end of December 1998;

- inform LEAs of the number of numeracy consultant posts the DfEE can guarantee to fund from 1 April 1999, asking them to recruit by the end of December to have them in post by 1 April 1999;

- begin work on the production of a specification for training courses; and

- begin to consider whether and how a standing committee for mathematics education might complement existing mechanisms.

autumn term 1998

- prepare training programmes and materials for inducting consultants and preparing "leading mathematics teachers" for their role;

- begin development work on materials for three day training courses, and distance learning materials for whole school INSET, particularly video material to show successful teaching of the daily mathematics lesson;

- consider the scope for including an element of STA training in funding for the National Numeracy Strategy, at the latest for 2000-2001;

- as part of the Standards Fund bidding process, agree targets for Key Stage 2 mathematics, and local action plans to improve standards of mathematics, with all LEAs, to include their plans for phasing of support for all schools and particularly those to receive intensive support;

- invite bids from LEAs to run pilot programmes for improving and extending numeracy skills at Key Stage 3;

- provide induction for Regional Directors of the strategy;

- continue to develop and expand the database of good practice and materials on the National Grid for Learning, to support effective teaching of mathematics;

- start planning for the World Mathematical Year 2000, beginning dialogue in particular with key players and local networks in the National Year of Reading; and

- give priority to supporting EAZ bids that put forward creative ideas for engaging the whole community in improving children's standards of numeracy, and the numeracy skills of adults, addressing in particular the need for participation from families that have not readily engaged with local schools.

spring term 1999

- send copies of the *Framework for teaching* to all teachers in primary, middle and special schools, LEAs, at least one copy to all secondary schools, and a reasonable number of copies to all ITT providers, ensuring that a continuing supply is printed;

- fund training for people identified to take up numeracy consultant posts and for the "leading mathematics teachers" who will support schools when the strategy begins, the training to be run in regions by the strategy's Regional Directors;

- organise conferences for LEA advisory and support staff to familiarise them with the training materials and discuss the support they will need to provide for consultants and schools;

- prepare training materials and programmes for the 5 day training courses for schools receiving intensive support;

- ensure that the guidance, training and support for the strategy helps teachers to teach the daily mathematics lesson to classes with a high proportion of pupils with SEN, EAL pupils, in small schools and with exceptionally able pupils; and

- include guidance on good practice in homework activities to support mathematics for children of different ages in the training and support materials, and a specific session on homework activities in the training materials developed to support the 5 day course for schools receiving intensive support.

summer term 1999

- start to develop the *Framework for teaching* into Year 7, working closely with QCA;

- with the TTA, hold regional conferences for INSET and ITT providers to familiarise them with the strategy, particularly the Framework; and

- consult on adding an "average level score" for primary pupils at the end of Key Stage 2 to future school performance tables for mathematics.

autumn term 1999

- with the TTA, draw up plans to facilitate the continuing professional development of teachers in mathematics;

- distribute leaflets to supermarkets and similar outlets, developed with QCA and the Basic Skills Agency, building on what the NNP and Hamilton Maths Project have already done, covering:

  - a general introduction to the importance of numeracy and the role parents can play;
  - the sorts of things children should be able to do at the end of each school year; and
  - activities for parents and children appropriate to children's different ages.

- make these leaflets available to after school childcare facilities to ensure that these staff, as well as parents, are fully informed;

- make further guidance on good practice in mathematics homework activities available on the National Grid for Learning; and

- ensure that the investment in study support facilities for all ages takes account of the importance of developing and practising numeracy skills.

spring term 2000

- prepare and distribute guidelines and training materials for LEAs about conferences for secondary heads of mathematics.

summer term 2000

- fund conferences for secondary heads of mathematics and persons in charge of liaison with primary schools to prepare them for the first intake of pupils from primary schools to have experienced the numeracy strategy.

LEAs should:

summer 1998

- work with schools to make continuous improvements to the arrangements for transfer of pupils between primary and secondary schools.

autumn term 1998

- identify mathematics co-ordinators and other teachers who have a particular strength in teaching mathematics who can act as "leading mathematics teachers", to support schools when the strategy begins;

- ensure that they have in post someone with the management experience and mathematical skills to line manage consultants and provide extra support for training;

- advertise for, and recruit, numeracy consultants in line with DfEE guidelines, by the end of December 1998, to take up post from 1 April 1999;

- liaise with the DfEE and consultants' existing employers to secure sufficient release for them in the spring term to undertake induction training;

- agree a Key Stage 2 mathematics target for 2002, and an action plan for raising standards of numeracy, with the DfEE; and

- build up and organise existing clusters and other local networks of schools, and encourage new ones, with a view to creating opportunities for sharing good practice.

spring term 1999

- assist the DfEE's Regional Directors in running and supplementing training for the numeracy consultants who will start work in April, and for the "leading mathematics teachers";

- negotiate and agree Key Stage 2 mathematics targets with schools, that will feed into the LEA target;

- send line managers and support staff to the DfEE conferences on the Numeracy Strategy; and

- identify the schools that will need the most intensive support in the first year of the strategy.

summer term 1999

- facilitate arrangements for teachers to watch demonstration lessons taught by a consultant or a "leading mathematics teacher";

- run three day conferences for headteachers, mathematics co-ordinators, one other teacher, and a governor, from all primary and special schools; and

- delegate funds to schools to spend on classroom resources for mathematics, in accordance with their audited needs.

summer term 2000

- run conferences about the strategy for secondary heads of mathematics.

Primary and middle schools and, where appropriate, special schools, should:

autumn term 1998

- if they have not already done so, identify a teacher who will act as mathematics co-ordinator, who should take advantage of any suitable training or briefing opportunities that come up in the time leading up to the strategy implementation, and take responsibility, with the headteacher, for familiarising themselves with the National Numeracy Strategy; and

- begin to build up a stock of number games that families can borrow to use at home.

spring term 1999

● agree a Key Stage 2 mathematics target for 2002 with their LEA; and

● further familiarise themselves with the National Numeracy Strategy, particularly the *Framework for teaching mathematics*, and QCA exemplification materials and guidance on the development of mental calculation strategies as they are received by schools.

summer term 1999

● send the headteacher, mathematics co-ordinator and one other experienced teacher who should usefully be the SENCO on the initial 3 day training course, with a governor attending for at least the third day;

● audit their current practice in mathematics, including classroom resources, to support the introduction of the daily mathematics lesson, and spend any Standards Fund grant delegated from the LEA accordingly;

● when auditing their mathematics provision, consider the extent to which they have suitable books and materials to support mathematics homework;

● devote one INSET day, after the initial training course, to a whole school training event to prepare for teaching the daily mathematics lesson the following term;

● involve adult helpers fully in preparation and training for the implementation of the National Numeracy Strategy;

● prepare medium term teaching plans for the autumn term and beyond, based on the yearly teaching programmes in the Framework; and

● prepare for, and start to use, the distance learning materials and QCA guidance on mental calculation.

autumn term 1999

● begin to teach the daily mathematics lesson for all pupils of between 45 minutes and one hour, depending on children's ages;

● devote an INSET day early in the term to further training on the daily mathematics lesson;

● early in the term, facilitate observation of demonstration lessons, either "live" or on video;

- establish the daily mathematics lesson in all classrooms, and begin to allow time for the mathematics co-ordinator and, where appropriate, other colleagues, to work with teachers to implement changes in practice, as deemed necessary on the basis of school review;

- ensure that suitable assessment procedures are in place to inform everyday teaching;

- provide, where possible and practical, the SENCO with time to work with the mathematics co-ordinator and other colleagues to implement the strategy within the school;

- schools receiving intensive support to send the mathematics co-ordinator and another teacher on a further course;

- arrange open evenings and other opportunities to tell parents about the teaching methods they will be using as they implement the National Numeracy Strategy, and how they can help their children develop good numeracy skills; and

- begin to set regular mathematical activities or exercises for all children to do at home with their parents.

spring and summer terms 2000

- devote another INSET day to further training to improve the daily mathematics lesson; and

- continue to ensure that the mathematics co-ordinator and, where appropriate, other colleagues, have time to work with colleagues in the classroom (e.g. by teaching demonstration lessons) to sustain the successful implementation of the daily lesson.

Mathematics teachers in secondary schools should:

spring term 1999

- familiarise themselves with the National Numeracy Strategy, including the structure and requirements of the *Framework for teaching*.

autumn term 1999

- plan and provide recovery programmes for Key Stage 3 pupils who have attained level 3 or below at Key Stage 2, focusing on mental calculation skills and strategies based on the *Framework for teaching*.

summer term 2000

- attend conferences about the National Numeracy Strategy to prepare for the first intake of pupils to have been taught the daily mathematics lesson in line with the National Numeracy Strategy.

autumn term 2000

- receive, and begin to teach, the first intake of Year 7 pupils who have experienced the National Numeracy Strategy; and

- plan for their own, and colleagues' continuing professional development needs in mathematics.

QCA should:

autumn term 1998

- ensure that the revised National Curriculum for mathematics emphasises oral and mental work in Key Stages 1 and 2, and that formal written work builds upon these secure foundations;

- take account of the structure and approach of the revised *Framework for teaching* when making changes to the National Curriculum for mathematics so that it is easy for teachers to see how the Framework is used to plan, and teach, the curriculum requirements; and

- in the review of the Desirable Learning Outcomes, seek to make more explicit the relative emphasis to be given to personal and social skills, and the specific skills needed in mathematics.

spring term 1999

- publish guidance on mental calculation strategies and on how calculators can be most effectively and sensibly used, that is specifically related to the revised *Framework for teaching*;

- publish exemplification material to help teachers monitor pupils' progress towards the teaching objectives in the *Framework for teaching*; and

- prepare advice on written calculation, which could usefully be included with the distance learning materials to be distributed to schools in summer 1999.

TTA should:

summer 1998

- ensure that national standards for headteachers, subject leaders and SENCOs take account of their respective roles in developing numeracy skills.

autumn term 1998

- consider the possibility of needs assessment material for non-specialist mathematics teachers at Key Stage 3.

spring term 1999

- consider how the developing plans for World Mathematical Year 2000 can be used to reinforce recruitment strategies for mathematics teachers.

OFSTED should:

autumn term 1998

- provide guidance for inspectors on inspecting numeracy, to be subsequently made available to schools.

summer term 1999

- run training for inspectors about the National Numeracy Strategy.

autumn term 1999

- undertake visits to a significant sample of schools to begin the evaluation of the strategy.

The Basic Skills Agency should:

- continue to publish *Count and Figure It Out Together*, as a continuing resource to support home numeracy activities with younger children, taking into account the objectives for these children in the National Numeracy Strategy; and

- extend and develop the Family Numeracy programme, building on the lessons of the 1998 pilot, aiming for maximum cost effectiveness and links to children's progress in the school curriculum.